California

Bed & Breakfast
Cookbook

From the

Warmth and

Hospitality of

California

Bed & Breakfast Inns

EXPANDED
2nd edition
New Inns
New Recipes

9   8   7   6   5   4   3   2

Second Edition
ISBN 978-1-889593-21-0
PUBLISHED BY:
3D Press
a Big Earth Publishing company
3005 Center Green Drive, Suite 220
Boulder, CO 80301

800-258-5830 (order toll free)
303-443-9687 (fax)
www.bigearthpublishing.com

FRONT COVER PHOTOS
   top: courtesy of Seven Gables Inn; **bottom:** courtesy of Inn Light Marketing
BACK COVER PHOTOS
   top & bottom: Applewood Inn, photo courtesy of Inn Light Marketing; **middle:** Ballard Inn
COVER AND TEXT DESIGN: Rebecca Finkel
EDITING: Becky LeJeune
PRINTED IN China by Imago

The Bed & Breakfast Cookbook Series was originated by Carol Faino & Doreen Hazledine of Peppermint Press in Denver, Colorado in 1996.

Introduction

The California Association of Bed & Breakfast Inns (CABBI) welcomes you to a taste of California. Encompassed in this cookbook, you'll find all the delectable sensations of California cuisine.

From spicy south-of-the-border influences, to time-honored recipes from Sierra mining towns, to wine country creations, or fresh seafood from the California coast, an epicurean experience at a CABBI bed and breakfast inn is long remembered.

Each recipe in this book was carefully chosen to tell the story of the inn from where it is served. Some recipes are house specialties, others are family traditions. Some dishes include locally-grown ingredients from an inn's region, while other dishes are the reason guests return time and again. The bed and breakfast inn was born of sharing food with friends. We hope that you will enjoy these CABBI favorites with your friends and loved ones, as we do with ours.

We look forward to welcoming you to a CABBI bed and breakfast inn.

Bon appétit,
THE MEMBERS OF THE
CALIFORNIA ASSOCIATION OF BED & BREAKFAST INNS

CALIFORNIA ASSOCIATION OF BED & BREAKFAST INNS
A non-profit trade organization

CABBI represents certified bed and breakfast inns throughout California as the largest bed and breakfast association in the United States. All CABBI inns are inspected and certified to meet quality standards. For more information on CABBI bed and breakfast travel, please visit us on the web at www.cabbi.com.

California

The word California is said to come from the story of an ancient land, a paradise populated by Amazons and ruled by Queen Califia. According to the legend, the kingdom ruled by Califia was said to be rich in gold and inhabited by a host of mythical creatures.

On January 24, 1848, gold was discovered at Sutter's Mill in Coloma, California. This was the beginning of the California Gold Rush, an era that would change the face of California forever. Over the years, the population of the state exploded with people hoping to find their fortune. This trend continues even today.

California is fairly young, having become the 31st state of the nation in 1850. The Golden State is the third largest state, after Texas and Alaska, and has the highest population in all of the U.S. Geographically, California is very diverse possessing everything ranging from beaches and mountains to desert and forests. In fact, over one-third of the state consists of forest-land that is home to some of the most endangered, as well as some of the world's largest, and oldest trees.

Today, California is known to the world as the center of the entertainment and music industries. Some of the United States' most recognizable landmarks - the Golden Gate Bridge and the giant Hollywood sign - can both be found within its borders. With its diverse population and its plethora of natural resources, the state also continues to maintain a top position in U.S. agricultural production and technological advances.

STATE SYMBOLS

STATE ANIMAL: Grizzly Bear

STATE BEVERAGE: Wine

STATE BIRD: California Valley Quail

STATE COLORS: Blue & Gold

STATE FISH: California Golden Trout

STATE FLOWER: Golden Poppy

STATE GEMSTONE: Blue Diamond

STATE INSECT: California Dogface Butterfly

STATE MARINE MAMMAL: California Gray Whale

STATE REPTILE: Desert Tortoise

FAMOUS CALIFORNIANS

Julia Child

John Frémont

William Randolph Hearst

Jack London

James W. Marshall

Marilyn Monroe

John Muir

Upton Sinclair

Leland Stanford

Johns Steinbeck

GEOGRAPHICAL FEATURES OF NOTE

Death Valley, second lowest point and hottest place in the Western Hemisphere

Mount Whitney, elevation 14,505 feet, highest point in contiguous U.S.

San Andreas Fault, approximately 800 miles long

National parks include Yosemite National Park, Joshua Tree National Park, and Redwood National Park

California Department of Parks and Recreation is responsible for over 270 protected areas, including state parks, campsites and trails

Hyperion, world's tallest tree at 379.1 feet, can be found in Redwood National Forest

Contents

Breads & Muffins

Breads & Muffins

"*Without bread all is misery.*"

—WILLIAM COBBETT

SECRET GARDEN
INN & COTTAGES

Secluded beneath high hedges, hidden pathways and romantic gardens, lies the Secret Garden Inn & Cottages. Built for a large family in 1905, the house is now a delightful inn. Enjoy the Mediterranean climate while indulging in a leisurely breakfast served in bed, on the privacy of your garden patio or beneath the lacy, intertwined branches of the persimmon and avocado trees.

Delicious buffet breakfasts include freshly baked scones and muffing, special fruit dishes and quiches.

INNKEEPER:	Dominique Hannaux
ADDRESS:	1908 Bath Street, Santa Barbara, California 93101
TELEPHONE:	(805) 687-2300; (800) 676-1622
E-MAIL:	garden@secretgarden.com
WEBSITE:	www.secretgarden.com
ROOMS:	11 Rooms; 3 Suites; 9 Cottages; Private baths
CHILDREN:	Welcome
PETS:	Welcome; Call ahead

Persimmon & Orange Nut Bread

Makes 2 Loaves

"We have a persimmon tree in the garden,
and our guests love it when we cook with the fresh persimmons.
This bread can be stored in the freezer for up to two months."

—Innkeeper, *Secret Garden Inn & Cottages*

3½ cups all purpose flour
2 cups brown sugar
2 teaspoons baking powder
1 teaspoon baking soda
½ teaspoon salt
1½ teaspoons cinnamon
½ teaspoon nutmeg
3 eggs
1 cup vegetable oil
½ cup orange juice
½ cup grated orange zest
2 cups persimmon pulp*
1 cup golden raisins
1 cup chopped nuts

Preheat oven to 325°F. In a large bowl, combine flour, brown sugar, baking powder, baking soda, salt, cinnamon and nutmeg. In a medium bow, beat together eggs, oil, orange juice, orange zest and persimmon pulp. Add egg mixture to flour mixture; stir until combined. Stir in raisins and nuts. Pout batter into 2 well greased 9x5-inch loaf pans. Bake for 50 minutes, or until a toothpick inserted in the center comes out clean. Cool on a wire rack.

Note: Persimmons are available from October to February.

Oak Hill Manor

The Oak Hill Manor, built in 1984, is a 6,000-square-foot home that has been completely renovated by innkeepers Maurice and Risë Macaré. This elegant inn contains five suites, each with a fireplace and a whirlpool or claw-foot tub. Common areas include a formal parlor, pub, library, sunroom, steam bath and other luxury amenities.

Innkeeper Risë Macaré decorated each suite using unique European country styles. The inn was honored for having the "Best Interior Design and Décor" in Arrington's Bed & Breakfast Journal's 200 Book of Lists.

INNKEEPERS:	Maurice & Risë Macaré
ADDRESS:	12345 Hampton Court, Atascadero, California 93422
TELEPHONE:	(805) 462-9317; (866) 625-6267
E-MAIL:	macare@oakhillmanor.com
WEBSITE:	www.oakhillmanor.com
ROOMS:	5 Suites; Private baths
CHILDREN:	Welcome
PETS:	Not allowed; Resident pet

Butterscotch Banana Bread

Makes 2 Loaves

"This delicious recipe is adapted from the Toll House Heritage Cookbook. *The recipe can easily be halved."*
—INNKEEPER, *Oak Hill Manor Bed & Breakfast*

2 cups mashed ripe banana (about 4-6 bananas)
1½ cups sugar
1 stick butter, melted
2 large eggs
3½ cups all-purpose flour
4 teaspoons baking powder
1 teaspoon baking soda
1 teaspoon cinnamon
1 teaspoon salt
1 teaspoon nutmeg
½ cup milk
2 ⅔ cups chopped pecans, divided
1 (12 ounce) package Nestlé butterscotch morsels

Preheat oven to 350°F. In a large bowl, cream together bananas, sugar, butter and eggs. In a small bowl, combine flour, baking powder, baking soda, salt, cinnamon and nutmeg. Gradually add flour mixture alternately with milk to banana mixture, mixing well after each addition. Stir in 2 cups of pecans and butterscotch morsels.

Divide batter between 2 greased and floured 9x5-inch loaf pans. Sprinkle with remaining ⅔ cup of pecans. Bake for 60–70 minutes, until a toothpick inserted in the center comes out clean. Cool bread in pans for 15 minutes then remove from pans to a wire rack.

THE INN AT LOCKE HOUSE

The Inn at
Locke House
Bed and Breakfast

Enjoy the romantic, simple elegance and serenity of the historic Inn at Locke House, a rural home graced with English country gardens. From your room, gaze upon the Sierra Foothills and countryside dotted with horse ranches, orchards and vineyards. Locke House is convenient to Lake Tahoe, Sierra Nevada resorts, Gold Country and Yosemite National Park.

   A freshly baked "confection of the day," a variety of delectable nibbles and beverages welcome guests to the inn. Later, join the innkeepers for dessert in the parlor, carriageway or farmhands' dining room.

INNKEEPERS:	Richard & Lani Eklund
ADDRESS:	19960 Elliot Road, Lockeford, California 95237
TELEPHONE:	(209) 727-5715
E-MAIL:	lockhouse@jps.net
WEBSITE:	www.theinnatlockehouse.com
ROOMS:	4 Rooms; 1 Suite; Private bats
CHILDREN:	Welcome; Call ahead
PETS:	Call ahead

Meyer Lemon Ginger Coffee Bread

Makes 1 Loaf

"Meyer lemons abound in our garden and I am always looking for ways to use this delightful, almost sweet, citrus fruit ... Guests enjoy the sweet tartness of this bread toasted and s pread with butter or softened cream cheese (to which I sometimes add a tiny bit of finely chopped crystallized ginger)."

— INNKEEPER, *The Inn at Locke House*

4 ripe Meyer lemons
2½ cups unbleached all-purpose flour
2 teaspoons double-acting baking powder
1 teaspoon baking soda
1 teaspoon ground ginger
½ teaspoon salt
1½ cups white sugar
2 large eggs
½ cup unsalted butter, melted
½ cup chopped pecans
½ cup finely chopped crystallized ginger

Preheat oven to 350°F. Grease one Danish loaf pan and set aside. Juice 2 of the lemons to make about ½ cup of juice; set juice aside and reserve peels. Cut the remaining 2 lemons into quarters and remove seeds. Place lemon quarters, juice and reserved peel in a food processor or blender and process until a smooth purée is formed. There should still be evidence of lemon peel and pulp.

In a medium bowl, sift flour with baking powder, baking soda, ground ginger and salt. In a large bowl, combine sugar, eggs and butter. Beat until smooth. Add lemon mixture and dry ingredients to sugar mixture. Mix together just until blended. Stir in pecans and crystallized ginger. Pour into loaf pan, smoothing top. Bake 40-45 minutes, or until a toothpick inserted in the middle comes out clean. Cool for 10 minutes and then remove from pan. Cool bread completely before cutting.

INN AT PLAYA DEL REY

Overlooking the sailboats of a main channel of Marina Del Rey and set on 300 acres of natural marshes is a place where life seems simpler. Recently named by Forbes.com as "One of the Nation's Top Ten Urban Inns," the Inn at Playa Del Rey is a New England-style beach house ideally located just three blocks from the ocean and 15 minutes from Manhattan Beach, Venice Beach and Santa Monica.

The inn's romantic suites are rich in sumptuous detail and feature Jacuzzi tubs, fireplaces, marina views, balconies and king-size canopy feather beds.

INNKEEPER: Liz Hall

ADDRESS: 435 Culver Boulevard, Playa Del Rey, California 90293

TELEPHONE: (310) 574-1920

E-MAIL: info@innatplayadelrey.com

WEBSITE: www.innatplayadelrey.com

ROOMS: 21 Rooms; Private baths

CHILDREN: Welcome

PETS: Not allowed

Low-Fat Honey Apricot Bread

Makes 3 Loaves

1 tablespoon butter
1½ cups sugar
3 eggs
6 egg whites
1 cup milk
1½ cups honey
1½ teaspoons vanilla extract
5 cups flour
1 tablespoon baking powder
1 tablespoon baking soda
2½ cups dried apricots, diced

Preheat oven to 350°F. Liberally spray 3 loaf pans with non-stick cooking spray. In a large bowl, cream together butter and sugar. Add beaten eggs and egg whites, milk, honey and vanilla to sugar mixture. Mix until well combined. In a medium bowl, mix together flour, baking powder and baking soda. Add flour mixture to sugar mixture, beat until smooth. Fold in diced apricots. Divide dough into 3 loaf pans and bake 45-60 minutes, or until a toothpick inserted in the middle comes out clean.

ROSE MOUNTAIN MANOR

Set on five wooded acres in historic Colfax, Rose Mountain Manor is filled with charm and small town atmosphere. Located in the Sierra Foothills, the inn is within a 15-minute drive of Auburn, Grass Valley and Nevada City. Escape from life's daily stresses with home-style hospitality in quiet, luxurious accommodations.

Away from the hustle and bustle, you'll find the quaint Victorian tearoom or the garden gazebo is the perfect place to enjoy a fine cup of tea and homemade scones and tea bread.

INNKEEPER:	Barbara Bowers
ADDRESS:	233 Plutes Way, Colfax, California 95713
TELEPHONE:	(530) 346-0067; (866) 444-7673
E-MAIL:	innkeeper@rosemountainmanor.com
WEBSITE:	www.rosemountainmanor.com
ROOMS:	3 Rooms; Private baths
CHILDREN:	Children age 10 and older welcome
PETS:	Not allowed

Strawberry Tea Bread

Makes 1 Loaf

½ cup butter, softened
1 cup sugar
½ teaspoon almond extract
2 eggs
2 cups flour
1 teaspoon baking powder
1 teaspoon baking soda
1 (10-ounce) package frozen strawberries,
    thawed and drained, juice reserved

Preheat oven to 350°F. Lightly grease a 9x5-inch loaf pan. In a large bowl, cream together butter, sugar and almond extract. Separate eggs and beat in egg yolks one at a time until mixture is light and fluffy. Sift flour, baking powder and baking soda into creamed mixture and mix thoroughly. Stir in ¼ cup of strawberry juice. Fold in strawberries. In a medium bowl, beat egg whites until stiff. Fold into strawberry batter. Turn batter into prepared pan. Lightly drop pan to pop any air bubbles. Bake 50-60 minutes, or until a toothpick inserted in the middle comes out clean. Cool bread before slicing.

BARNEY'S
RANCHO BERNARDO

Barney's Rancho Bernardo Bed & Breakfast is a 40-acre cattle ranch located in secluded Cathey's Valley. Expansive vistas of rolling hills dotted with ancient oak trees, Chinese rock walls, springs and grazing livestock surround the ranch and guest houses, making Rancho Bernardo more like a resort than a bed & breakfast.

Rancho Bernardo is ideally located near Yosemite National Park, the ghost town of Hornitos, Lakes Bagby and McClure, gold panning, skiing, river rafting on the mighty Merced River and a host of other activities.

INNKEEPERs:	Kathleen & Barney Lozares
ADDRESS:	2617 Old Highway South, Cathey's Valley, California 95306
TELEPHONE:	TELEPHONE:(209) 966-4511; (877) 930-1669
E-MAIL:	Kathleen@ranchobernardobnb.com
WEBSITE:	www.ranchobernardobnb.com
ROOMS:	1 Suite; 1 Guest House; Private baths
CHILDREN:	Children age 8 and older welcome
PETS:	Not allowed; Resident horses and pets

The Best Zucchini Bread Ever

Makes 2 Loaves

"This bread is extremely moist and delicious.
It was adapted from Teri's Recipe Page at Epicurious.com."

~ INNKEEPER, *Barney's Rancho Bernardo Bed & Breakfast*

4 large eggs
4 cups shredded zucchini, with skins
3 cups flour
2½ cups sugar
1½ cups vegetable oil
1 tablespoon plus 1 teaspoon vanilla extract
2 teaspoons cinnamon
1½ teaspoons salt
1½ teaspoons baking soda
½ teaspoon cloves
½ teaspoon baking powder
1 cup walnuts, chopped

Preheat oven to 325°F. Generously grease the bottom of 2 9x5-inch loaf pans. In a large bowl, beat the eggs. Add the remaining ingredients without beating between additions. Beat all ingredients with an electric mixer at low speed for 1 minute, scraping sides of bowl often. Divide batter evenly between loaf pans. Bake 1 hour 15 minutes. Remove from oven and allow to cool, in pans, for 10 minutes. Slide a metal spatula or knife between the side of the pan and the bread to separate before removing. Cool on wire rack before slicing.

SHAW HOUSE B&B INN

Built in 1854 by the city's founder for his bride, the Shaw House Bed & Breakfast Inn, the oldest bed & breakfast in California, served as the first courthouse and post office in Ferndale. This Carpenter Gothic Revival house is a rare find with its jutting gables, balconies and bay windows. A one-acre cottage garden surrounds this beautiful home in a timeless, park-like setting.

Fresh fruit and flowers garnish morning culinary treats such as mushroom leek frittata, French bread pudding with homemade berry sauce, cheddar Parmesan strata, crêpes, scones and homemade bread.

INNKEEPER: Paula Bigley

ADDRESS: 703 Main Street, Ferndale, California 95536

TELEPHONE: (707) 786-9958; (800) 557-7429

E-MAIL: stay@shawhouse.com

WEBSITE: www.shawhouse.com

ROOMS: 6 Rooms; 2 Suites; Private baths

CHILDREN: Welcome

PETS: Pets under 50 pounds welcome; Resident pets

Shaw House Bread

Makes 8 Servings

"This recipe never fails to please guests. It has endless variations –
substitute blueberries, apples, cherries and chocolate or raspberries."

—INNKEEPER, *Shaw House Inn*

6–7 frozen croissants
¼ cup whipped cream cheese
½ cup diced dried apricots
¼ cup sliced almonds
3 cups half & half
4 eggs
⅓ cup sugar
2 teaspoons almond extract

APRICOT SAUCE
2 can apricots in pear juice
⅓ cup sugar
Dash nutmeg or allspice
1 tablespoon cornstarch, diluted with water for thickening

Spray a 9x13-inch baking dish with non-stick cooking spray.
Cut croissants into bite-sized pieces and fill baking dish to top.
Tuck cream cheese between croissant pieces. Sprinkle apricots and
almonds around croissants. Use a blender to whip together half
& half, eggs, sugar and almond extract. Pour mixture over top of
croissants. Refrigerate overnight.

Preheat oven to 350°F. Remove refrigerated bread and bake in
oven 50-55 minutes. Top with apricot sauce to serve.

For apricot sauce: In a small saucepan over medium heat, bring
canned apricots and sugar to a boil. Reduce heat to simmer and
stir in diluted cornstarch and nutmeg. Cook, stirring often, until
thickened.

CARRIAGE VINEYARDS B&B

Situated on a 100-acre ranch near Paso Robles, Carriage Vineyards Bed & Breakfast is ideal for those seeking a peaceful country retreat. The inn's name is derived from the property's vineyards and the innkeepers' carriage collection.

Wander amidst 20,000 grape vines planted on 27 acres. The inn is home to 500 olive trees and a 2,400-square-foot carriage house sheltering 12 antique carriages. Relax with a book under a tree in the small orchard or find peace of mind in the vegetable garden, flower gardens and sitting areas.

INNKEEPERS:	Leigh Anne & Joe Farley
ADDRESS:	4337 South El Pomar Road, Templeton, California 93465
TELEPHONE:	(805) 227-6807; (800) 617-7911
E-MAIL:	stay@carriagevineyards.com
WEBSITE:	www.carriagevineyards.com
ROOMS:	4 Rooms; Private baths
CHILDREN:	Children age 10 and older welcome
PETS:	Not allowed

Barbecued Olive Bread

Makes 2 Loaves

*"We have approximately 500 olive trees on the property.
This bread, which is actually grilled, is a way to use
some of our annual olive harvest."*

—INNKEEPER, *Carriage Vineyards Bed & Breakfast*

1 (4-ounce) can chopped ripe olives
½ cup chopped pimento-stuffed olives
¾ cup grated Colby Jack cheese
½ cup plus 4 tablespoons grated
   Parmesan cheese, divided
½ stick butter, melted
1 tablespoon olive oil
2 cloves garlic, minced
3 drops hot pepper sauce
2 cups biscuit mix (such as Bisquick)
²/₃ cup milk
2 tablespoons minced fresh parsley
Paprika

Preheat grill. In a small bowl, combine ripe and pimento-stuffed olives, Colby Jack cheese, ½ cup Parmesan cheese, melted butter, olive oil, garlic and hot pepper sauce; set aside.

In a medium bowl, combine biscuit mix, milk, 2 tablespoons of Parmesan cheese and parsley; stir until moist, then press into 2 (9-inch) disposable aluminum pie pans. Top dough with olive mixture. Sprinkle with paprika and remaining 2 tablespoons of Parmesan cheese.

Grill bread over indirect heat, covered, for 8-10 minutes, or until crust is golden brown when edge of bread is lifted with a spatula.

GLENDEVEN INN

A stay at the Glendeven Inn offers guests the opportunity to get away from it all - to relax in the refreshing peace and natural beauty of its elegant surroundings. Casual elegance abounds in the airy and spacious guest rooms, each one different from the next but all incorporating fine antiques with specifically selected contemporary art. Glendeven is the perfect place whether you are looking to bask in the beauty of California's North Coast, enjoy the many outdoor activities of the area or just enjoy a romantic retreat with that special someone.

"Thank you for a wonderful stay and a chance to share the beauty of Glendeven. The experience of waking up and looking out to the Pacific, blue jays at your window, and a floral path to add color to your day ... and of course the 4-star breakfast basket, is beyond words!"
— Guest

INNKEEPER: John Dixon

ADDRESS: 8205 North Highway One, Little River, California 95456

TELEPHONE: (800) 822-4536

E-MAIL: innkeeper@glendeven.com

WEBSITE: www.glendeven.com

ROOMS: 10 Rooms; 6 Suites; 1 Barn Loft; Private baths

CHILDREN: Children ages 16 and older welcome

PETS: Not allowed; Resident pets

Etta's Cornbread

Makes 9 Servings

"Emily Etta Stevens Pullen, the fourth daughter of Isaiah Stevens who built the farmhouse which is now Glendeven Inn's main building, kept a diary beginning in 1864, when she and her family made the daring voyage from Maine to Little River, until 1935, tow years before her death. A copy of Etta's lifelong diary is kept in one of Glendeven's rooms, aptly named 'Etta's Suite.' Etta lived in Little River until her death at 83 years old. This is her recipe for corn bread."

—INNKEEPER, *Glendeven Inn*

1 cup flour
¾ cup yellow cornmeal
½ cup grated Pepper Jack cheese
1 teaspoon baking powder
1 teaspoon salt
2 eggs
1 cup milk
3 tablespoons honey
½ stick unsalted butter, melted

Preheat oven to 425°F. Generously spray an 8x8-inch baking dish with non-stick cooking spray. In a large bowl, combine flour, cornmeal, cheese, baking powder and salt. In a medium bowl, whisk together eggs, milk and honey; add to dry ingredients. Stir melted butter into batter. Bake 15-20 minutes.

OLD YACHT CLUB INN

Santa Barbara's beautiful East Beach is one block from the Old Yacht Club Inn. East Beach was rated one of the world's ten

best beaches by the L.A. Times. Beach chairs, towels and bikes are provided by the inn.

Saturday dinner has been an Old Yacht Club tradition since 1980. Guests gather for champagne and are then seated for a five-course, prix fixe menu. The entrée typically incorporates the freshest and best fish available that day. Recipes such as artichokes Athena, salmon with raspberry buerre blanc sauce and chocolate cheesecake showcase the chef's talent.

INNKEEPERS:	Eilene Bruce & Vince Pettit
ADDRESS:	431 Corona Del Mar Drive, Santa Barbara, California 93103
TELEPHONE:	(805) 962-1277; (800) 676-1676
E-MAIL:	info@oldyachtclubinn.com
WEBSITE:	www.oldyachtclubinn.com
ROOMS:	14 Rooms; 1 Suite; 1 Cottage; Private baths
CHILDREN:	Welcome
PETS:	Not allowed

Old Yacht Club Inn Beer Bread

Makes 1 Loaf

3 cups self-rising flour
1 (8-ounce) can beer
½ cup half & half or milk
2 tablespoons sugar
½ stick butter, melted

Preheat oven to 325°F. In a large bowl, combine flour and sugar. In a small bowl, mix together beer and half & half. Add beer mixture to flour mixture, stir together until fully incorporated (dough will be quite sticky). Place dough in a greased and floured 9x5x3-inch butter loaf pan. Poke holes in top of dough and drizzle with butter*. Bake 1 hour. Let cool before slicing.

Note: Butter overflows while baking, place loaf pan on a baking sheet while cooking to avoid mess.

Did you know that the type of beer you use will effect the type of bread you get? A darker beer will result in a darker bread just as a lighter ale will result in a lighter bread.

MISSION INN
SAN JUAN CAPISTRANO

The Mission Inn is an early California, Hacienda-style inn nestled in the coastal Capistrano Valley between the Pacific Ocean and the Cleveland National Forest. The inn sits on a two acre, century-old family orchard adjacent to the historic Mission San Juan Capistrano. The melodic sound of the mission's bells can be heard while strolling through historic San Juan, as you read by the inn's pool or sip sherry on the veranda.

Patio rooms have a patio for private outdoor lounging under one of the orchard's orange trees – you can pick a fresh orange any time you desire!

INNKEEPERS: Harold & Sunshyne Croucher
ADDRESS: 26891 Ortega Highway, San Juan Capistrano, California 92675
TELEPHONE: (949) 234-0249; (866) 234-0249
E-MAIL: innkeeper@missioninnsjc.com
WEBSITE: www.missioninnsjc.com
ROOMS: 18 Rooms; 2 Suites; Private baths
CHILDREN: Children age 12 and older welcome
PETS: Welcome

Sarah's Mississippi Buttermilk Biscuits

Makes 8 Large or 10 Small Biscuits

2 cups self-rising all-purpose flour
1 cup buttermilk
½ cup canola oil
Butter or margarine, for serving
Preserves or honey, for serving

Preheat oven to 400°F. Mix flour, buttermilk and oil until moist. Roll out dough and cut with a biscuit cutter or glass. Place biscuits in a cast-iron skillet or greased baking pan. Bake for 20 minutes, or until tops are golden brown. Serve piping hot with butter or margarine and your favorite preserves or honey.

In the South, biscuits are most often served with gravy. Most popular is white, or country, gravy made with sausage. Another interesting variety is red eye gravy made with coffee.

THE INN AT SCHOOLHOUSE CREEK

Experience the true luxury of solitude at this Mendocino Coast inn. Set on eight acres of ocean-view gardens, meadows, forest and a secluded beach cove, you will truly feel like you've gotten away from it all. The Inn at Schoolhouse Creek offers privacy and a carefree atmosphere where you can enjoy your vacation on your own schedule. Sit in the gardens or watch the waves break and the whales spout from your cottage.

The charming and historic village of Mendocino, with its many fine shops, galleries and restaurants, is five minutes from the inn.

INNKEEPERS:	Steven Musser & Maureen Gilbert
ADDRESS:	7051 North Highway One, Mendocino, California 95456
TELEPHONE:	(707) 937-5525; (800) 731-5525
E-MAIL:	innkeeper@schoolhousecreek.com
WEBSITE:	www.schoolhousecreek.com
ROOMS:	4 Rooms; 2 Suites; 9 Cottages; Private baths
CHILDREN:	Welcome
PETS:	Welcome; Resident pets

Apple Cheddar Muffins with Rosemary

Makes 12 Muffins

1½ cups all-purpose flour
¼ cup old-fashioned rolled oats
1 tablespoon sugar
2 teaspoons baking powder
½ teaspoon baking soda
½ teaspoon salt
⅛ teaspoon white pepper
⅛ teaspoon cardamom
¼ teaspoon allspice
½ teaspoon minced fresh rosemary
¾ cup skim milk
2 eggs, beaten
½ stick unsalted butter, melted
1 large Granny Smith or pippen apple,
    peeled and cut into 1/8-inch dice
¾ cup grated sharp white cheddar cheese

Preheat oven to 400°F. In a large bowl, combine flour, oats, sugar, baking powder, baking soda, salt, white pepper, cardamom, allspice and rosemary. In a medium bowl, whisk together milk, eggs and melted butter. Stir apples and cheese into egg mixture. Add egg mixture to flour mixture and stir just until blended.

Pour batter into greased muffing cups. Bake for 15-20 minutes, or until a toothpick inserted into center comes out clean. Cool muffins in pan for 3 minutes, then remove to a wire rack.

STRAWBERRY CREEK INN

The tranquil and rejuvenating setting of the Strawberry Inn is the perfect place to get away from it all and relax. Each room at the Strawberry Creek Inn has been uniquely designed to offer guests a comforting stay that is both peaceful and elegant. Each visit to Strawberry Creek includes their signature organic breakfast made from fresh-produce and local ingredients. To add that special touch to your stay, Strawberry Creek Inn also offers guests the option of including champagne or flowers and chocolates in your room.

Idyllwild, named one of the best 18 cities in California, maintains that small-town charm while offering a plethora of activities. It's a great place for enjoying outdoor activities such as fishing, hiking and rock climbing. Or you can indulge in more leisure activities like antique shopping, scenic mountain drives and wine tasting. In the evening, treat yourself to dinner at one of the town's award winning restaurants before returning to the

INNKEEPERS: Rodney & Ian Williams

ADDRESS: 26370 Highway 243, Idyllwild, California 92549

TELEPHONE: (951) 659-3202; (800) 262-8969

E-MAIL: innkeeper@strawberrycreekinn.com

WEBSITE: www.strawberrycreekinn.com

ROOMS: 9 Rooms; 1 Cottage; Private baths

CHILDREN: Welcome

PETS: Not allowed; Resident pets

Carrot Cake Muffins

Makes 12 Muffins

"Like their namesake cake, these muffins will transport you back to your grandmother's kitchen. Perfect served with eggs and fresh fruit."

—INNKEEPER, *Strawberry Creek Inn*

1¾ cups all-purpose flour
1 teaspoon baking powder
¾ teaspoon baking soda
1 teaspoon cinnamon
½ teaspoon kosher salt
¾ cup whole plain yogurt
1 tablespoon vanilla extract
2 ounces olive oil
10 ounces sugar
3 large eggs
3–4 raw carrots, grated
1⅓ cups toasted walnuts, chopped
⅔ cup rum soaked raisins*

Preheat oven to 350°F. In a large bowl, sift together flour, baking powder, baking soda, cinnamon and salt. In a separate medium bowl, whisk together yogurt, vanilla extract, olive oil, sugar and eggs. Add wet mixture to dry mixture, mixing until just combined. Fold in carrots, walnuts and raisins. Using an ice-cream scoop, scoop muffin batter into a well-buttered or sprayed muffin pan; batter should just reach the tops of the muffin tin. Place muffin pan on center oven rack and bake 25 minutes, or until a toothpick inserted in the center comes out clean. Allow to cool before removing from muffin tins and serving.

For raisins: Pour 2 tablespoons rum over dry raisins and add enough hot water to cover. Soak 15 minutes; pour off water and allow raisins to dry.

HENNESSEY HOUSE B&B

A stay at the charming and elegant Hennessey House Bed & Breakfast will leave guests feeling as if they have stepped back in time. Dr. Edwin Hennessey, a noted and successful physician,

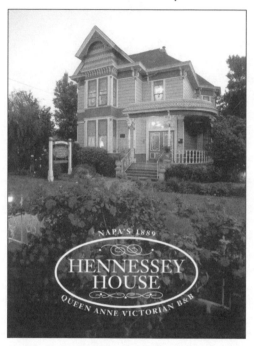

and his family built this "painted lady" in 1889. Today, the home is listed on the National Register of Historic Places. Owners Kevin and Lorri Walsh purchased the home in 2004 and love blending the warmth and welcome of Victorian times with discreetly placed modern amenities.

All rooms at the Hennessey House come with private baths and custom bath accessories, featherbeds outfitted in luxury linens, sherry and chocolates. Gourmet breakfast, afternoon refreshments and evening wine and cheeses are served daily.

INNKEEPERS: Kevin & Lorri Walsh

ADDRESS: 1727 Main Street, Napa, California 94559

TELEPHONE: (707) 226-3774

E-MAIL: inn@hennesseyhouse.com

WEBSITE: www.hennesseyhouse.com

ROOMS: 10 Rooms; Private baths

CHILDREN: Welcome

PETS: Not allowed

Pineapple Ricotta Muffins

Makes 12 Muffins

"Top with granola or butter-nut crumble topping
before baking for an interesting variation. Delicious!"

—INNKEEPER, *Hennessey House Bed & Breakfast*

1 egg
Vegetable oil
1½ cups Ricotta cheese
1 cup crushed pineapple
2 cups flour
½ cup sugar
1 tablespoon baking powder
½ teaspoon baking soda
½ teaspoon salt

Preheat oven to 350°F. Break egg into a measuring cup and add enough vegetable oil to make ½ cup. Measure Ricotta cheese into a large mixing bowl and add egg/oil mixture; mix well. Stir in crushed pineapple. In a medium bowl, sift together the dry ingredients; add to the cheese mixture, stirring just until the flour mixture is absorbed. Scoop mixture into lined muffin tin and bake 20-25 minutes.

OLD ST. ANGELA INN

The Old St. Angela Inn, born a country home in 1910 and converted to a rectory and then a convent in 1920, is now a cozy bed & breakfast inn overlooking Monterey Bay. Within this turn-of-the-century, shingle-style home are rooms of distinctive individuality and warmth that provide comfort and serenity.

The Old St. Angela Inn is conveniently located just 100 yards from the water and only minutes from excellent restaurants and shopping, world-class golf, Monterey's Old Cannery Row and the Monterey Bay Aquarium.

INNKEEPERS:	Jerry & Dianne McKneely
ADDRESS:	321 Central Avenue, Pacific Grove, California 93950
TELEPHONE:	(831) 372-3246; (800) 748-6306
E-MAIL:	Dianne@oldstangelainn.com
WEBSITE:	www.oldstangelainn.com
ROOMS:	9 Rooms; Private baths
CHILDREN:	Children age 6 and older welcome
PETS:	Not allowed

Blueberry Crunch Muffins

Makes 15 Regular Muffins or 12 Extra Large Muffins

"We get many requests for these muffins."

—INNKEEPER, *Old St. Angela Inn*

TOPPING:
½ cup flour
½ cup sugar
½ cup butter, softened

MUFFINS:
3 cups flour
1 cup sugar
4 teaspoons baking powder
1 teaspoon salt
2 eggs, beaten
1 cup milk
½ cup butter, melted
2 teaspoons vanilla extract
2 cups fresh blueberries (can use frozen)

Preheat oven to 350°F. In a small bowl, combine topping ingredients until crumbly; set aside. In a large bowl, combine flour, sugar, baking powder and salt. In a medium bowl, mix together eggs, milk, butter and vanilla extract. Stir egg mixture into flour mixture just until dry ingredients are moistened. Stir in blueberries. Spoon batter into muffin tins, about ⅔ full, and sprinkle topping evenly over each muffin. Bake 20-25 minutes until lightly browned and a toothpick inserted in the center comes out clean.

UNION STREET INN

Experience warm European hospitality in San Francisco's elegant Union Street Inn. Combining the elegance and gentility of an Edwardian home, the inn is the perfect pied-à-terre for those wanting to explore San Francisco. Rooms are spacious, airy and comfortably furnished. Antique accents, fresh flowers and pleasing artworks create a sense of the romantic.

Open the window and the fragrance of old roses, lavender, sage and rosemary wafts up from the cottage garden – a delightful spot to enjoy a delectable breakfast or afternoon tea.

INNKEEPERS: Jane Bertorelli & David Coyle

ADDRESS: 2229 Union Street, San Francisco, California 94123

TELEPHONE: (415) 346-0424

E-MAIL: innkeeper@unionstreetinn.com

WEBSITE: www.unionstreetinn.com

ROOMS: 6 Rooms; Private baths

CHILDREN: Welcome

PETS: Not allowed; Resident pets

Raspberry Almond Muffins

Makes 12 Jumbo Muffins

3 cups all-purpose flour
$^2/_3$ cup sugar
1 teaspoons salt
1 teaspoons baking powder
1 teaspoons baking soda
2 cups raspberries
2 large eggs
2 tablespoons almond extract
¼ cup canola oil
1¼ cups buttermilk (about)
Sliced almonds

Preheat oven to 375°F. Line 12 jumbo muffin cups with paper liners or spray with non-stick cooking spray. In a bowl, combine flour, sugar, salt, baking powder and baking soda. Gently stir in raspberries.

Beat eggs in a 2 cup measuring cup. Mix almond extract and oil into eggs. Add enough buttermilk to egg mixture to make 2 cups of liquid. Add egg mixture to flour mixture; stir gently just until combined. Divide batter among muffin cups. Sprinkle with almonds. Bake for 30 minutes, until firm to the touch.

UPHAM HOTEL

The Upham Hotel & Cottage Gardens is situated on an acre of gardens in the heart of downtown Santa Barbara, a red tile, white adobe, flower-decked town evoking romanticized Spanish California. The hotel is the oldest continuously operating hostelry in Southern California. *San Francisco Focus* magazine awarded the Upham Hotel its California Grand Hotel Award for the "Best Small Hotel in Southern California." Louie's, the hotel's restaurant, features California's cuisine and has been nationally recognized by *Travel & Leisure* magazine.

INNKEEPER:	Jan Martin Winn
ADDRESS:	1404 De La Vina Street, Santa Barbara, California 93101
TELEPHONE:	(805) 962-0058; (800) 727-0876
E-MAIL:	innkeeper@uphamhotel.com
WEBSITE:	www.uphamhotel.com
ROOMS:	37 Rooms; 5 Suites; 8 Cottages; Private baths
CHILDREN:	Welcome
PETS:	Not allowed

Almond Joy Muffins

Makes 12 Muffins

2 eggs
½ cup sugar
½ cup butter, room temperature
¾ cup milk
1⅓ cups flour
1½ teaspoons baking powder
½ teaspoon baking soda
¼ teaspoon salt
1½ cups coconut
½ cup chocolate chips
½ cup sliced almonds

Preheat oven to 350°F. In a large bowl, combine eggs, sugar, butter and milk. In a medium bowl, sift together flour, baking powder, baking soda and salt. Add flour mixture to egg mixture, mixing well until fully combined. Stir in coconut, chocolate chips and almonds. Line a muffin pan with muffin cups and scoop in dough – the cups should be about ⅔ filled. Sprinkle additional coconut over the top of each muffin. Bake for 20 minutes.

Banana Coconut Bread with Lemon Glaze

Makes 1 Loaf

2 cups flour
¾ teaspoon baking soda
½ teaspoon salt
1 cup sugar
¼ cup butter, softened
2 eggs
1½ cups mashed banana (about 3)
¼ cup sour cream
2 tablespoons vanilla extract
½ cup flaked coconut
1½ tablespoons lemon juice
½ cup powdered sugar

Preheat oven to 350°F. In a medium bowl, whisk together flour, baking soda and salt. Place sugar and butter in a large mixing bowl and beat with an electric mixer on medium speed, until well blended. Add eggs 1 at a time, beating well after each addition. Add bananas, sour cream and vanilla and mix until blended. Add flour mixture; beat at low speed just until moist. Stir in the coconut. Spoon the batter into a greased 9x5-inch loaf pan. Sprinkle top with an additional 2 tablespoons of coconut and bake 1 hour, or until a toothpick inserted in the center comes away clean. Cool in pan for 10 minutes on a wire rack. Remove from pan and brush with lemon glaze.

For glaze: In a small bowl, combine lemon juice and sugar, stirring until mixture is fully combined.

Swirled Pound Cake

Makes 1 Cake

1 cup butter

2 cups granulated sugar

6 eggs

1 cup sour cream

3 teaspoons baking powder, sifted

3 cups flour

1 teaspoon vanilla extract

3 tablespoons unsweetened cocoa powder

½ cup chocolate chips

½ cup chopped nuts

COCOA GLAZE:

1 cup powdered sugar

2½ tablespoons unsweetened cocoa powder

2–3 tablespoons milk

Preheat oven to 300°F. Thoroughly grease a 10-inch fluted tube pan. In a 5-quart mixing bowl, cream butter and sugar until light and fluffy. Add eggs one at a time and beat well after each addition. In a separate bowl, sift together baking powder and flour. Alternately add flour mixture and sour cream to egg mixture, stirring until fully combined. Add vanilla extract and mix well. Spread ½ of the batter in the bottom of the prepared pan. Stir cocoa powder into the remaining batter. Stir in chocolate chips and nuts. Pour the chocolate batter evenly over the plain batter. Using a metal spatula, make a zigzag pattern in the batters. Bake 1 hour, or until a toothpick inserted in the center comes away clean. Remove and cool in pan for 10 minutes before removing. Allow cake to cool completely before drizzling with cocoa glaze.

For the glaze: In a medium bowl, mix together powdered sugar, unsweetened cocoa and enough milk to make a glaze of desired consistency. Glaze should be smooth and not too thin.

Coffee Cakes, Scones & Cereals

Coffee Cakes, Scones & Cereals

The fine arts are five in number, namely: painting, sculpture, poetry, music, and architecture, the principle branch of the latter being pastry.

—MARIE-ANTOINE (ANTONIN) CARÊME

APPLEWOOD INN

The relaxing and romantic Applewood Inn is hidden away in Sonoma County's Russian River Valley, on a knoll surrounded by tall redwoods. The inn consists of two types of accommodations. The cozy Belden House features 9 modest but comfortable rooms and a lounge with a river-rock fireplace that's the perfect place for

socializing with fellow guests. The remaining 10 rooms, all Mediterranean villa inspired in décor, can be found in the inn's newer buildings. The exceptional service, comforting atmosphere and rustic cuisine provided at the Applewood Inn have earned it rave reviews from travelers and guests and is a great place for a quiet, romantic vacation.

"We would like to thank both of you so much for the wonderful stay at your beautiful inn. The scenery and gardens were spectacular, the food was fabulous, our room was comfortable and cozy and the entire ambiance was delightful! It was a perfect spot for spending our 25th anniversary! Thanks for all the directions & suggestions of where to travel. … We certainly hope to return sometime in the near future."

—Guest

INNKEEPERS: Darryl Notter & Jim Caron

ADDRESS: 13555 Highway 116, Guerneville, California 95446

TELEPHONE: (707) 869-9093; (800) 555-8509

E-MAIL: relax@applewoodinn.com

WEBSITE: www.applewoodinn.com

ROOMS: 19 Rooms; Private baths

CHILDREN: Welcome

PETS: Dogs welcome; Resident pets

Applewood Inn's
Plum Upside-Down Coffee Cake

Makes 8 Servings

*"In the summer, Applewood's orchard of heritage fruit trees
produces an abundance of apples, pears, peaches, quince,
apricots, figs and plums. This coffee cake is a great way
to use out Santa Rosa plums and the guests love it.
Recipe adapted from Food and Wine Magazine."*

—INNKEEPER, APPLEWOOD INN

15 tablespoons unsalted butter	½ teaspoon salt
1 cup packed brown sugar	1 cup sugar
1 cup honey	3 large eggs
6 large plums, halved and pitted	1 teaspoon vanilla extract
1½ cups all-purpose flour	1 teaspoon almond extract
2 teaspoons baking powder	½ cup milk
½ teaspoon cinnamon	

Preheat oven to 350°F. Stir 9 tablespoons of butter, brown sugar
and honey in a heavy skillet until the butter melts and the sugar
and honey blend in. Transfer to a 9-inch cake pan. Arrange plum
halves cut-side-down over mixture. In a medium bowl, mix
together flour, baking powder, cinnamon and salt; set aside. In a
large bowl, beat the remaining 6 tablespoons of butter with sugar
until creamy. Add eggs one at a time and beat until mixture is light
and fluffy then beat in vanilla and almond extracts. Add dry ingredients alternately with milk, mixing until just blended. Spoon the
batter evenly over the plums. Bake 1 hour and 5 minutes, or until
golden and a toothpick inserted in the center comes out clean.
Transfer pan to a wire rack and allow to cool for 25 minutes.

Using a knife, cut around the side of the pan to loosen the cake.
Place a serving plate atop the cake pan and invert cake. Let cake
stand, still in pan, for 5 minutes then gently remove the pan.
Dust cake with powdered sugar and serve with whipped cream
or mascarpone sweetened with honey.

AUBERGE MENDOCINO

AUBERGE MENDOCINO

The Auberge Mendocino, overlooking Little River Bay on the rugged Northern California coast, offers comfort with style in a setting of exceptional beauty. Just outside historic Mendocino, the inn is nestled between two California state parks. Whale watching, hiking and water sports are at your door. The Mendocino Wine Country and Noyo Harbor sports are just a few miles down scenic California Highway One.

A scrumptious breakfast may include scrambled eggs with smoked salmon, home fries with dill rémoulade sauce, and boysenberry scone cake.

INNKEEPER:	Richard Grabow
ADDRESS:	8200 Highway 1, Little River, California 95465
TELEPHONE:	(707) 937-0088; (800) 347-9252
E-MAIL:	innkeeper@aubergemendocino.com
WEBSITE:	www.aubergemendocino.com
ROOMS:	11 Rooms; Private Baths
CHILDREN:	Welcome
PETS:	Pets welcome; Call ahead

Apricot Cream Cheese Coffee Cake

Makes 12 Servings

"This cake is also known as 'David's Cake,' named after my 5-year-old nephew who sad, 'This is the best cake I've ever eaten in my whole life!' This recipe is from Rachel's Heritage Collection, *a collection of recipes from the inn's former owner."*

— INNKEEPER, Auberge Mendocino

1 stick butter, softened
½ cup sugar
Grated zest of 1 lemon
2 large eggs
1 teaspoon vanilla extract
1 teaspoon baking powder
½ teaspoon salt
1 heaping cup unbleached all-purpose flour
10 apricots, halved and pitted (or plums)

TOPPING:
½ (8-ounce) package cream cheese, softened
½ cup sugar
2 tablespoons sour cream
1 large egg
1 teaspoon vanilla extract

Preheat oven to 350°F. In a large bowl, cream together butter, sugar and lemon zest. Beat in eggs, 1 at a time. Beat in vanilla. In a small bowl, combine baking powder, salt and flour; beat into butter mixture. Pour batter into a greased 9-inch springform pan. Place apricots skin-side-down on top of batter. Spread topping over apricots. Bake for 1 hour, or until top is set and begins to brown.

For the topping: Beat cream cheese and sugar until smooth. Add sour cream, egg and vanilla; beat well.

TIFFANY COUNTRY HOUSE

The Tiffany Country House is a striking Victorian mansion located on a tree-lined street. The inn is just a short walk from Santa Barbara and its museums, art galleries and restaurants. Luxurious bedrooms include queen-size beds, whirlpool baths and large, open windows. The penthouse suite is a gorgeous, full-floor room with a fireplace, private balcony and spectacular mountain views.

The Taste of Romance Package includes champagne and a gift certificate for dinner at Louie's, one of Santa Barbara's best-loved restaurants.

INNKEEPER: Jan Martin Winn

ADDRESS: 1323 De La Vina Street, Santa Barbara, California 93101

TELEPHONE: (805) 963-2283; (800) 999-5672

E-MAIL: frontdesk@tiffanycountryhouse.com

WEBSITE: www.tiffanycountryhouse.com

ROOMS: 7 Rooms; Private baths

CHILDREN: Children age 16 and older welcome

PETS: Not allowed

Sour Cream Banana Toffee Crumb Cake

Makes 1 Cake

"This recipe is adapted from one in Food & Wine *magazine. It is simple and delicious."*

—INNKEEPER, *Tiffany Country House*

2¾ cups all-purpose flour
2½ teaspoons baking powder
½ teaspoon baking soda
½ teaspoon salt
1½ stick butter, softened
1½ cups sugar
3 large eggs
1½ teaspoons vanilla extract
1 cup sour cream
½ cup mashed ripe banana

TOFFEE TOPPING:
½ cup coarsely chopped chocolate-covered
   English toffee (such as Skor or Heath bar)
⅓ cup all-purpose flour
¼ cup powdered sugar
2 tablespoons butter

Preheat oven to 350°F. In a medium bowl, whisk together flour, baking powder, baking soda and salt. In a large bowl, beat butter and sugar with a mixer until light and fluffy. Beat in eggs and vanilla. Beat in sour cream and banana until smooth. Beat in flour mixture until smooth.

Pour batter into a greased, 10-inch springform pan. Sprinkle toffee topping over batter. Bake for 70 minutes, or until a toothpick inserted in the center comes out clean. Cool cake slightly in pan, then remove outer rim from pan and cool cake completely.

For the toffee topping: Combine topping ingredients until crumbly.

THE J. PATRICK HOUSE

This charming, Irish inspired bed & breakfast sits in the heart of Cambria. Voted the Best B&B on the West Coast by Inn Traveler Magazine, the J. Patrick House offers guests a friendly and relaxing atmosphere with indulgent amenities. The authentic log cabin houses an elegant guest suite and the carriage house is home to seven cozy, country style guest rooms.

"My wife and I spent our 15th anniversary in JPH last November and are so looking forward to doing them same on our 16th this November. A beautiful room, great hosts, superb dining and chocolate chip cookies with milk in front of a roaring fire … sublime! We especially enjoyed gathering around the main living room with you and the other guests. You truly have created something special in Cambria and I can't think of a better place to begin each Holiday season." —Guest

INNKEEPERS: Ann O'Connor & John Arnott

ADDRESS: 2990 Burton Drive, Cambria, California 93428

TELEPHONE: (805) 927-6759; (800) 341-5258

E-MAIL: jph@jpatrickhouse.com

WEBSITE: www.jpatrickhouse.com

ROOMS: 8 Rooms; Private baths

CHILDREN: Children age 14 and older welcome

PETS: Not allowed

English Scones

Makes 16 Scones

½ cup dried cranberries

2 tablespoons brandy

1 teaspoon grated orange peel

4 cups all-purpose flour

¾ cup sugar

2 tablespoons baking powder

½ teaspoon salt

2 sticks cold unsalted butter, or margarine

1 cup buttermilk

Preheat oven to 400°F. In a small microwave-safe bowl, combine cranberries, brandy and orange peel; microwave for 25 seconds. In a large bowl, combine flour, baking powder and salt. Cut in the butter and mix until dough consists of ¼-inch lumps. Stir in cranberry mixture. Add buttermilk and stir. If dough is crumbly, add addition buttermilk and stir. Put dough on a wooden board and knead until it holds together. Form dough into a ball and cut in half. Shape each half into a ½-inch thick round and place on a cookie sheet. With a floured knife, cut each round into eighths. Brush tops of rounds with 2 tablespoons of buttermilk and baked 25-30 minutes, until scones are golden brown. Transfer to a wire rack and allow to cool before serving.

CHANNEL ROAD INN

The Channel Road Inn provides the comfortable elegance of a turn-of-the-century Santa Monica home and the timeless pleasure of a seashore retreat. This fully restored, circa 1915 manor is located only one block from the glorious Santa Monica beach in Santa Monica Canyon, an exclusive, yet eclectic and rustic section of Los Angeles.

When you are ready to re-join the pulse of the city, some of the area's best dining, shopping and entertainment are within five minutes. Ride, jog or walk south to the Santa Monica Pier, or drive along the coast to Malibu.

INNKEEPER: Christine L. Marwell

ADDRESS: 219 West Cannel Road, Santa Monica, California 90402

TELEPHONE: (310) 459-1920

E-MAIL: info@channelroadinn.com

WEBSITE: www.channelroadinn.com

ROOMS: 14 Rooms; 1 Suite; Private baths

CHILDREN: Welcome

PETS: Not allowed

Cream Scones with Berries

Makes 12 Scones

2 cups all-purpose flour
1 tablespoon sugar, plus extra for topping
1 tablespoon baking powder
1 stick butter, chilled an cut into small pieces
2 eggs
½ cup heavy cream
1½ teaspoons vanilla extract
1 cup fresh or frozen berries of choice
Egg wash (1 egg yolk beaten with
    1 tablespoon of water or milk)

Preheat oven to 350°F. In a large bowl, combine flour, sugar and baking powder. Cut in butter until mixture resembles a coarse meal. In a medium bowl, combine eggs, cream and vanilla. Stir cream mixture into flour mixture until flour is incorporated, then mix for 1-2 minutes longer. Add berries and mix gently just until combined.

With an ice cream scoop, scoop batter onto a parchment paper-lined baking sheet. Brush scones with a little egg wash and sprinkle with sugar. Bake 30-40 minutes, or until golden brown on top.

CAPAY VALLEY B&B

Just a short drive from the Bay Area and Sacramento, the Capay Valley Bed & breakfast sits peacefully surrounded by fountains and private sanctuaries. With over 70 animals on this 142-acre property, guests can take part in farm activities, adventures or just lounge by the pool.

Capay Valley offers the ultimate in casual relaxation. Play croquet, Bocci and horseshoes on the grassy lawn. Or head out on the hiking and biking trails or a horseback ride – bike rentals and horse boarding available.

INNKEEPER: Elizabeth Campbell
ADDRESS: 15875 State Highway 16, Capay, California 95607
TELEPHONE: (866) 227-2922
E-MAIL: capayinn@mac.com
WEBSITE: www.capayvalleybedandbreakfast.com
ROOMS: 4 Rooms; 2 Cottages; Private & shared baths
CHILDREN: Call ahead
PETS: Call ahead

World Famous Scones

Makes 10 to 12 Scones

"These scones are our signature dish. People just rave about them!"

—INNKEEPER, *Capay Valley Bed & Breakfast*

3 cups all-purpose flour
¼ teaspoon salt
⅓ cup white sugar
1½ sticks butter
2½ teaspoons baking powder
½ teaspoon baking soda
Grated zest and juice of 1 lemon
Grated zest of 1 orange
1 cup milk
¼ cup whipping cream
1 cup raisins or dried cherries or
   cranberries (or a mixture)
½ cup raw sugar
2 teaspoons cinnamon

Preheat oven to 450°F. In a food processor, pulse together flour, salt, white sugar, butter, baking powder, baking soda, lemon zest and orange zest.

In a small bowl, combine milk, cream and lemon juice; add to flour mixture in food processor. Add raisins and process until blended.

On a floured surface, roll dough out ⅓-inch thick. Cut dough with a medium or large biscuit cutter. Sprinkle with raw sugar and cinnamon. Bake on a greased cookie sheet for 15-18 minutes, or until golden brown.

ALEGRIA OCEANFRONT INN & COTTAGES

A legria, which means the state of being joyful and happy, is an inn that welcomes you by putting your cares to rest and applying attention to every detail of your stay. The innkeepers want you to focus on more important things – the hummingbird out the window, the fragrance of the ocean breeze, or the sunlight across the garden path leading to the beach.

Breakfast is served each morning in the ocean-view dining room. Offerings, which incorporate organic products when possible, include vanilla pecan waffles, pumpkin ginger pancakes, or blueberry cream cheese coffee cake.

INNKEEPERS:	Eric and Elaine Wing Hillesland
ADDRESS:	44781 Main Street, Mendocino, California 95460
TELEPHONE:	(707) 937-5150; (800) 780-7905
E-MAIL:	inn@oceanfrontmagic.com
WEBSITE:	www.oceanfrontmagic.com
ROOMS:	8 Rooms; 2 Suites; 4 Cottages; Private baths
CHILDREN:	Welcome
PETS:	Not allowed

Orange Cranberry Chocolate Chip Toasted Walnut Scones

Makes 22 Scones

"These scones took 1st place at the Mendocino County Fair in 2005. Eric and Elaine's daughter, Tavi, who was 8-years-old at the time, entered her Buttermilk Biscuits in the adult division because she missed the deadline for the kid's division. Tavi won 1st Place beating her mom, a victory almost as delicious as her biscuits."

—INNKEEPER, *Alegria Oceanfront Inn & Cottages*

1 egg	1 teaspoon baking soda
1½ cups buttermilk	1 teaspoon salt
2 teaspoons vanilla extract	½ cup sugar
Zest of ½ an orange	1¼ cups chilled butter (2½ sticks)
(about 1 teaspoon)	1 cup dried cranberries*
4 cups flour	1 cup toasted walnuts or almonds
4 teaspoons baking powder	½ cup chocolate chips

Preheat oven to 425°F. In a medium bowl, beat together egg, buttermilk, vanilla extract and orange zest. Place flour, baking powder, baking soda, salt and sugar in a large bowl or food processor. Cut in chilled butter. If using food processor, transfer mixture to a large bowl after mixing in butter. Add wet mixture to dry mixture and mix together (with a tossing motion) until a loose, soft dough forms. Fold in cranberries, walnuts and chocolate chips. Scoop dough out onto greased baking sheets with an ice cream scoop placing scones about 1½-inches apart. Brush with cream and sprinkle with raw sugar. Bake 15-17 minutes.

To Freeze: Scoop dough onto an ungreased baking sheet that will fit in your freezer. After frozen solid, store in a hard plastic container up to one month in the freezer. To bake, place scones on greased cookie sheet and let them thaw about 20 minutes before putting them into preheated 375°F oven.

Optional: In a saucepan, bring dried cranberries and ¼ cup cointreau (or orange juice with a splash of brandy) to a boil. Remove from heat and let sit for 5 minutes. Drain cranberries before adding to dough.

ANDERSON CREEK INN

In a lovely valley near the Mendocino Coast, you will find the Anderson Creek Inn. This gracious, ranch-style inn sits on 16 acres near the town of Boonville. The inn tastefully blends the beauty of the Anderson Valley with warm hospitality.

Breakfasts feature homemade baked goods and memorable entrées such as croissant French toast with raspberries, blackberries and mandarin oranges or baked bananas with Chantilly cream. After breakfast, stroll around the lovely garden or treat yourself to an in-room massage.

INNKEEPERS:	Jim & Grace Minton
ADDRESS:	12050 Anderson Valley Way, Boonville, California 95415
TELEPHONE:	(707) 895-3091; (800) 552-6202
E-MAIL:	innkeeper@andersoncreekinn.com
WEBSITE:	www.andersoncreekinn.com
ROOMS:	5 Rooms; Private baths
CHILDREN:	Children age 10 and older welcome
PETS:	Not allowed; Resident pet

Buttermilk Scones

Makes 12 Scones

*"These scones are always a hit with our guests and won
a 1st place ribbon at the Mendocino County Fair in 2007."*
—INNKEEPER, *Anderson Creek Inn*

3 cups all-purpose flour
½ cup sugar
2½ teaspoons baking powder
½ teaspoon salt
¾ teaspoon kosher salt
¾ cup cold unsalted butter, cut into small pieces
¾ cup dried blueberries
Grated peel of one lemon
1 cup buttermilk
1 tablespoon cream,
1 egg yolk
2 tablespoons cinnamon/sugar mixture

Preheat oven to 375°F. In a large bowl, stir together flour, sugar,
baking powder, baking soda and salt until thoroughly blended.
Using a pastry blender, cut butter into flour mixture until it
resembles course cornmeal; stir in blueberries and lemon peel.
Make a well in the center of the flour mixture; add buttermilk
all at once. Stir mixture with a fork until the dough cleans the
sides of the bowl.

With your hands, gather the dough into a ball; turn dough lightly
onto a floured board. Pat into a 1-inch thick log and cut into triangles. Place 1½ inches apart on a baking sheet lined with parchment paper. In a small bowl, whisk together cream and egg yolk.
Brush tops of scones with cream mixture, then sprinkle heavily
with cinnamon/sugar mixture. Bake 20 minutes, or until tops are
lightly browned.

BISSELL HOUSE

During the late 19th century, Pasadena's Orange Grove Avenue was lined with beautiful mansions, some of which still stand. Built in 1887, the Bissell House Bed & Breakfast has been the southern anchor of this famous street, which was traditionally referred to as "Millionaire's Row."

"A beautiful home filled with care and attention.
It was a pleasure to stay where we were made to feel welcome
and pampered. Our room was large, beautifully decorated, with a large
closet and lovely, old-fashioned bath. We couldn't have been happier."
—Guest

INNKEEPER:	Juli Hoyman
ADDRESS:	201 Orange Grove Avenue South, South Pasadena, CA 91030
TELEPHONE:	(626) 441-3535; (800) 441-3530
E-MAIL:	info@bissellhouse.com
WEBSITE:	www.bissellhouse.com
ROOMS:	7 Rooms; Private baths
CHILDREN:	Children age 10 and older welcome
PETS:	Not allowed

Raspberry Pikelets with Mascarpone

Makes 4 Servings

"This is a favorite with our guests!
It was adapted from the book, Breakfasts by Jacque Malouf."
—INNKEEPER, *The Bissell House*

TOPPING:
5 ounces mascarpone
¼ teaspoon vanilla extract
2 tablespoons
   confectioner's sugar

PIKELETS:
4 tablespoons yogurt
4 tablespoons milk

Grated zest of 1 lemon
2 extra-large eggs
3 tablespoons sugar
2 tablespoons melted butter
1¼ cups all-purpose flour
1 teaspoon baking powder
Pinch of sea salt
½ cup raspberries or blueberries

For topping: In a medium bowl, beat all topping ingredients together until smooth. Cover and refrigerate until ready for use.

For the pikelets: In a medium bowl, whisk together yogurt, milk, lemon zest, egg yolks, sugar and melted butter until smooth. Set aside for 10 minutes. In a separate bowl, beat egg whites until stiff. Sift together flour, baking powder and salt; add to yogurt mixture mixing until well combined. Gently fold fruit into batter, followed by egg whites. Cook 2 tablespoons of batter in a heated skillet or griddle with butter, 1-2 minutes per side. Serve 3 pikelets with a topping of mascarpone and berries for color.

THE WINE COUNTRY INN
& GARDENS

T he Wine Country Inn & Gardens, Napa Valley's first bed & breakfast, has been transformed into a sensuous boutique hotel that offers a tranquil setting and luxurious accommodations. The splendid location offers guests a breathtaking view of the surrounding hills, mountains, vineyards and farmhouses. Magnificent gardens encompass the Wine Country Inn. Follow the cobbled pathways through 80-year-old olive trees, grand old oaks, flowerbeds, scrub and creeping vines.

Enjoy a complimentary gourmet breakfast each morning. The inn also offers a daily appetizer hour that features breads, assorted dips and a local wine selection. Indulge yourself and take advantage of the inn's signature spa service while you stay and sign up to take part in inn's olive oil making workshop hosted by innkeeper Jim Smith.

INNKEEPER:	Jim Smith
ADDRESS:	1152 Lodi Lane, St. Helena, California 94574
TELEPHONE:	(707) 963-7077; (888) 465-4608
E-MAIL:	romance@winecountryinn.com
WEBSITE:	www.winecountryinn.com
ROOMS:	20 Rooms; 4 Suites; 5 Cottages; Private baths
CHILDREN:	Welcome
PETS:	Not allowed

Granola

Makes 4 Servings

"We have been making and selling this granola daily for 32 years.
At Christmas time we mail pounds and pounds of it to our guests.
This was originated by a past employee."
—INNKEEPER, *The Wine Country Inn*

2 cups Quaker Old Fashion Oats
1 cup slivered almonds
¼ cup butter, melted
¼ cup honey
¼ cup brown sugar
Sprinkle of cinnamon
Dash of salt
1 cup flaked coconut
1 cup raisins

Preheat oven to 350°F. Mix together oats and almonds in a large baking pan. In a small bowl, stir together melted butter and honey. Pour over oats and mix well. Sprinkle brown sugar, cinnamon and salt over top. Stir.

Bake until golden brown, stirring regularly. Spread coconut over top and return to oven to bake until coconut is medium brown. Remove from oven and pour into a large bowl to cool. Stir regularly while cooling to prevent sticking. Once granola has completely cooled, stir in raisins and enjoy.

Granola is a most versatile food. It is commonly eaten with milk as a breakfast cereal, but can also be used as a topping for deserts and yogurt. It is also a popular hiking snack because it is high in energy, easy to store, and lightweight.

GOOSE & TURRETS

The inviting Goose & Turrets Bed & Breakfast was originally built in 1907. Over the years, the building has played host to a variety of businesses including Montara's first post office, a local grocery, a club for veterans of the Spanish American war, WWII housing for gunnery school officers and a music and dance school. Finally, in 1983, owners Emily and Raymond moved into the building and opened their bed & breakfast. Outside, the grounds consist of vegetable and herb gardens, orchards, flower gardens and fountains all surrounded by a massive 50-year-old Cypress hedge. Inside, there are 5 uniquely appointed guest rooms as well as spacious and comforting common areas.

Afternoon tea is served promptly at 4:30 every day and features an ever-changing variety of types of tea and accompanying dishes. Guests are also treated to a mouth-watering and always healthy 4-course breakfast. Though the menu changes daily, many of the ingredients come from the inn's own gardens.

INNKEEPER:	Emily Hoche-Mong
ADDRESS:	835 George Street, Montara, California 94037
TELEPHONE:	(650) 728-5451
E-MAIL:	rhmgt@montara.com
WEBSITE:	http://goose.montara.com
ROOMS:	5 Rooms; Private baths
CHILDREN:	Welcome
PETS:	Not allowed

Bellila – A Hot Cereal

Makes 2 Servings

*"My French husband spent his early years in Egypt.
This is a Middle Eastern recipe he often had at breakfast.
Plan ahead, this needs to be prepared the night before."*

—INNKEEPER, *Goose & Turrets Bed & Breakfast*

½ cup regular barley
Water
¼ cup sugar, or to taste
Milk

The night before, boil barley in enough water to cover. Remove from heat and allow to soak overnight.

In the morning, add sugar and milk. Stir well and cook in a saucepan over low heat. Let the mixture boil gently. Add water if the barley absorbs all of the liquid. Barley is ready when it is creamy and tender. Serve hot with a dash of spice (nutmeg, cloves or cinnamon).

Barley has been a staple food in Egypt, Greece and even Tibet for centuries. It has a wide variety of uses and is commonly found in cereals, soups and stews, can be ground into a flour, and is also a key ingredient in beer and whisky.

French Toast, Pancakes & Waffles

French Toast, Pancakes & Waffles

All happiness depends on a leisurely breakfast.

—John Gunther

Joshua Grindle Inn

The AAA Four-Diamond Joshua Grindle Inn is a beautiful 19th-century ocean-view home, surrounded by two acres of lush gardens. The inn offers the leisure and solitude you seek; yet it is an easy walk to everything in the village of Mendocino. Guests can hike the coast, browse the shops in Mendocino, horseback ride on the beach, read in the inn's gardens of dine in one of Mendocino's award-winning restaurants.

Amenities include luxurious robes and fine toiletries, such as locally made glycerin soaps, Mendocino Cookie Company cookies and Husch wines.

INNKEEPERS:	Charles & Cindy Reinhart
ADDRESS:	44800 Little Lake Road, Mendocino, California 95460
TELEPHONE:	(707) 937-4143; (800) 474-6353
E-MAIL:	stay@joshgrin.com
WEBSITE:	www.joshgrin.com
ROOMS:	8 Rooms; 2 Cottages; Private baths
CHILDREN:	Children age 12 and older welcome
PETS:	Not allowed; Resident pets

Cranberry Pumpkin French Toast

Makes 12 Servings

Plan ahead —
this French toast needs to be started the night before.

12 slices sourdough bread, cut into 1-inch cubes
1 (8-ounce) package cream cheese, cubed
1 (16-ounce) package fresh or frozen cranberries
   or 1 (16-ounce) can whole cranberries
12 large eggs
2 cups milk
2 cups canned pumpkin
1 tablespoon cinnamon
1 teaspoon ground cloves
1½ teaspoons ground ginger
1½ teaspoons nutmeg

CRANBERRY SAUCE:
1 (16-ounce) can jellied cranberry sauce
½ cup sugar, or to taste
½ cup water, about

Spray a 1-x15-inch baking pan with non-stick cooking spray. Place ½ of bread cubes in bottom of pan. Top with cream cheese. Top cream cheese with ¾ of cranberries. Top with remaining bread and cranberries.

Beat together eggs, milk, pumpkin, cinnamon, cloves, ginger and nutmeg; pour over bread. Cover with plastic wrap and press firmly so bread soaks up egg mixture. Refrigerate overnight.

The next day, preheat oven to 350°F. Bake French toast for 40 minutes (check after 25 minutes – if French toast is browning too quickly, cover with foil). Let stand 10 minutes. Slice and serve with cranberry sauce.

For the cranberry sauce: Heat cranberry sauce and sugar in saucepan over medium-low heat. Cook, stirring, until sugar dissolves. Thin with water to desired consistency.

CANDLELIGHT INN

BED & BREAKFAST

CANDLELIGHT INN

Napa Valley

Built in 1929 by the local postmaster, the Candlelight Inn is an exquisite example of English Tudor architecture. With white-washed plaster set between blackened oak timbers, the inn reflects light both inside and out. This exceedingly romantic and soothing environment is perfect for a visit to the Wine Country. Secluded beneath towering redwoods along the banks of Napa Creek, the inn sits on an acre of quiet, park-like grounds.

A three-course, gourmet breakfast, wine and hors d'oeuvres, elegant guestrooms and luxurious amenities make your stay one to remember.

INNKEEPER: Wendy Kelts

ADDRESS: 1045 Easum Drive, Napa, California 94558

TELEPHONE: (707) 257-3717; (800) 624-0395

E-MAIL: mail@candlelightinn.com

WEBSITE: www.candlelightinn.com

ROOMS: 10 Rooms; Private baths

CHILDREN: Call ahead

PETS: Not allowed; Resident pet

Croissant French Toast with Spiced Apples, Pears & Cranberries

Makes 12 Servings

SPICED APPLE, PEAR AND CRANBERRY TOPPING:
1½ cups frozen cranberries
1 teaspoon plus 1 tablespoon Grand Marnier
¾ cup loosely packed brown sugar, divided
¾ stick butter
4 medium Fuji apples, peeled and diced
4 medium Granny Smith apples, peeled and diced
6 Bartlett pears, peeled and diced
2–3 tablespoons cinnamon
⅛ teaspoon nutmeg
½ cup maple syrup

FRENCH TOAST:
2 cups half & half or cream
4 large eggs
1 tablespoon cinnamon
¼ cup powdered sugar, plus extra for garnish
24 mini or 12 large croissants, cut in half lengthwise

For the spiced apple topping: Combine cranberries, 1 teaspoon of Grand Marnier and 2 tablespoons of brown sugar in a saucepan over medium heat. Cook until cranberries are tender; set aside. Melt butter in a saucepan over medium heat. Add apples, pears, remaining brown sugar, cinnamon and nutmeg; cook for 5 minutes. Add 1 tablespoon of Grand Marnier and maple syrup; cook, stirring often, until fruit is tender. Remove from heat and stir in cranberry mixture.

For the French toast: Combine half & half, eggs, cinnamon and powdered sugar. Dip croissants into egg mixture. Cook on a hot, greased griddle or skillet until golden brown on both sides. Top with spiced apple topping and drizzle with pan juices. Dust with powdered sugar and serve.

VINE HILL INN

This award-winning, beautifully remodeled 1887 Victorian farmhouse is located in west Sonoma County. Nestled between vineyards and apple orchards in rural Sebastopol, this casual yet tasteful country inn is just one hour from San Francisco. Unwind in this idyllic country setting, where guests are pampered with delicious breakfasts, Egyptian cotton towels and glorious views from the decks and porches.

The inn's location is ideal for winery touring, exploring the Russian River or whale watching and swimming at nearby beaches.

INNKEEPER: Kathy Deichmann

ADDRESS: 3949 Vine Hill Road, Sebastopol, California 95472

TELEPHONE: (707) 823-8832

E-MAIL: reservations@vine-hill-inn.com

WEBSITE: www.vine-hill-inn.com

ROOMS: 4 Rooms; Private baths

CHILDREN: Call ahead

PETS: Small dogs welcome; Resident pet

Strawberry Croissant French Toast

Makes 8 Servings

8 croissants, halved lengthwise
1 (8-ounce) package cream cheese, softened
2 cups sliced strawberries, plus extra for garnish
3 large eggs
1 cup milk
1 teaspoon cinnamon
½ cup sugar
1 teaspoon nutmeg
1 teaspoon almond extract

Spread croissant bottoms with cream cheese. Top with strawberries, then sandwich with croissant tops. In a deep dish, beat together eggs, milk, cinnamon, sugar, nutmeg and almond extract. Dip croissants in egg mixture and cook on hot, buttered griddle or skillet until golden brown on both sides (be careful – croissants burn easily). Garnish with sliced strawberries to serve.

Note: This recipe can be easily halved – just use 2 eggs instead of 3.

Amorosa
Inn & Gardens

The Amorosa Inn & Gardens began life as the site of a 25-acre vineyard and winery. Owners Mike and Renae Matson added the custom-built four-bedroom home so that they might bring guests a relaxing bed & breakfast experience along with their distinctive Vino Con Brio wines. The combination is nothing less than a perfect vacation getaway for those looking for a little romance. Amorosa Inn & Gardens also provides a great home away from home for business travelers.

Rooms at the Amorosa Inn are exquisitely decorated in an eclectic blend of antique and contemporary furnishing. Guests can relax on their own veranda while tasting the local wine and enjoying the lush vineyard view.

INNKEEPER:	Renae Matson
ADDRESS:	7889 East Harney Lane, Lodi, California 95240
TELEPHONE:	(209) 368-5658: (888) 368-5658
E-MAIL:	renae@amoroainn.com
WEBSITE:	www.amorosainn.com
ROOMS:	3 Rooms; 1 Suite; Private Baths
CHILDREN:	Welcome
PETS:	Small dogs welcome; Call ahead

Stuffed Croissant French Toast

Makes 8 Servings

"Our guests' all-time favorite breakfast!"

—INNKEEPER, *Amorosa Inn & Gardens*

8 croissants, preferably 1 day old,
  halved lengthwise
4 eggs
½ cup milk
4 bananas, thinly sliced
2 teaspoons sugar
¼ teaspoon cinnamon
2 tablespoons butter
8 tablespoons cream cheese

For Stuffing: Put cream cheese into a microwave safe bowl and heat 20 seconds, or until softened. In a medium bowl, toss banana slices with cinnamon and sugar; set aside.

For French toast: In a large bowl, whisk together eggs and milk until blended. In a large skillet or griddle over medium heat, heat 2 tablespoons of butter until foam subsides. Quickly dip each croissant half into the egg batter then transfer to hot skillet with a slotted spatula; cook until golden brown, about 4 minutes on each side. Cook remaining croissants, adding butter as needed. Transfer cooked croissants to a large dish. Cover bottom slice of each croissant with 1 tablespoon of cream cheese, then a large spoonful of the cinnamon sugar bananas and cover with the top of the croissant. Serve immediately.

ARNOLD BLACK BEAR INN

T he Black Bear Inn is situated in a park-like setting and is comprised of several new timber-frame buildings that offer a lodge-like feel and an outdoorsy air. Centrally located near restaurants, antique shops, galleries, shopping, golf, skiing and wineries, the town of Arnold's only bed & breakfast is an ideal mountain getaway.

"Thank you for a wonderful time.
The rooms are very comfy — especially with all the bear accents.
The breakfast was out of this world! We will be back soon."
—Guest

INNKEEPERS: Doreen & Kirk Swanson

ADDRESS: 1343 Oak Circle, Arnold, California 95223

TELEPHONE: (209) 795-8999; (866) 795-8999

E-MAIL: innkeeper@arnoldblackbearinn.com

WEBSITE: www.arnoldblackbearinn.com

ROOMS: 5 Rooms; Private baths

CHILDREN: Cannot accommodate

PETS: Not allowed; Resident pets

Nut-Crusted French Toast

Makes 9 Servings

"This dish is why our own cookbook came to be!
It has become our signature dish and we serve it every Sunday
morning. This recipe was adapted from Oprah *magazine."*

—INNKEEPER, *Arnold Black Bear Inn*

1 loaf French bread, cut into ¾-inch slices
6 eggs
¾ cups whole milk
1 teaspoon vanilla
1 teaspoon cinnamon

NUT-CRUST TOPPING:
¾ cups brown sugar
¾ cups plain bread crumbs
¾ cups coarsely ground almonds

For French Toast: In a large bowl or electric mixer, combine eggs, milk, vanilla extract and cinnamon; set aside. Place some of the nut crust mixture on a large dinner plate. Dip a slice of the bread into the egg mixture and allow excess to drip off. Then, coat battered bread in nut mixture. Cook French toast on a hot griddle or skillet over medium-high heat with lots of butter, until toast is golden brown on both sides being careful not to let the almonds burn.

Serve with syrup and a dusting of powdered sugar.

For Topping: Mix all ingredients together and store in a tightly covered bowl

BEAZLEY HOUSE
B&B INN

Beazley House Bed & Breakfast Inn, located in the center of historic downtown Napa, is just steps from the trolley to COPIA, Victorian neighborhoods, the Napa River, gourmet restaurants and premium outlet shopping. Beazley House, with its central location for exploring wineries and the surrounding Wine Country, is the perfect Napa Valley bed & breakfast.

Elegant yet comfortable guest rooms have private baths and garden views. The romantic Carriage House offers true Napa-Style luxury with whirlpool tubs, fireplaces and complete privacy in hide-away rooms.

INNKEEPERS: Jim & Carol Beazley
ADDRESS: 1910 First Street, Napa, California 95449
TELEPHONE: (707) 257-1649; (800) 559-1649
E-MAIL: innkeeper@beazleyhouse.com
WEBSITE: www.beazleyhouse.com
ROOMS: 6 Rooms; 5 Suites; Private baths
CHILDREN: Welcome
PETS: Dogs welcome; Resident pets

Crème Caramel Overnight French Toast

Makes 9 Servings

"This delicious breakfast dish is one of the most popular and most requested dishes that we serve. It has evolved over the years to reflect our continuing efforts to provide healthy, delicious cuisine."

—INNKEEPER, *Beazley House Bed & Breakfast Inn*

CRÈME CARAMEL:
1 cup brown sugar
¼ cup butter
½ cup honey
1 tablespoon cinnamon
1 tablespoon nutmeg
2 tablespoons dried orange peel

1 loaf French bread, cut into 8–9 slices
1½ cups liquid egg substitute
2½ cups nonfat milk
⅓ cup sugar
1 tablespoon cinnamon
½ tablespoon ground allspice
1 tablespoon vanilla extract

Spray a 9½ x 13-inch baking dish with non-stick cooking spray. Mix Crème Caramel ingredients together in a small saucepan over low heat. Just when mixture is about to boil, turn off the heat and mix again thoroughly. While caramel is hot, pour into your baking dish and chill in the refrigerator for 10-20 minutes, or until set. You'll know it's ready when a light touch leaves your fingerprint on the caramel's surface.

Place sliced French bread in the baking dish over the caramel mixture. In a medium bowl, combine egg substitute, milk, sugar, cinnamon, allspice and vanilla extract. Pour mixture over bread. Cover dish and refrigerate overnight.

In the morning, preheat oven to 350°F. Bake French toast on top oven rack until set (approximately 1 hour).

When serving, flip pieces onto the plate so that the caramel sauce drips down over the toast. Top with fresh fruit and a dollop of low-fat yogurt to serve.

GOODMAN HOUSE

This 1906 home has seen many changes through the years. Once a residence, a law office and now a bed & breakfast, The Goodman House is one of Chico's Historic Landmarks. Margo and Tom Graham have tirelessly worked to restore the home to its original condition and opened for business in Spring of 2007. The elegant parlor features antique decorations and a baby grand piano. Each of the private rooms is outfitted with antique furnishings, queen beds, fine linens and down comforters as well as robes and fresh flowers. Some of the rooms' private baths even include claw foot tubs and three of the rooms also have their own fireplaces.

Guests can enjoy an early morning coffee on the front porch, read the paper and play board games in the upstairs lounge and enjoy a daily breakfast in the formal dining room. Hiking, biking, fishing, swimming, picnicking and horseback riding are just a few of the activities available just a walk away.

INNKEEPERS: Margo & Tom Graham
ADDRESS: 1362 Esplanade, Chico, California 95926
TELEPHONE: (530) 566-0256
E-MAIL: proprietor@goodmanhouse.net
WEBSITE: www.goodmanhouse.net
ROOMS: 5 Rooms; Private baths
CHILDREN: Welcome; Call ahead
PETS: Not allowed

Amaretto French Toast

Makes 6 Servings

*"Almonds are a major crop in Butte County and the recipe features
our favorite 'nut.' This recipe was published in Savor magazine."*
—INNKEEPER, *Goodman House Bed & Breakfast*

12 1-inch thick slices of dense textured bread
   such as Challah
6 eggs
2 cup half & half
⅓ cup plus 1 teaspoon Amaretto, divided
1 tablespoon honey
Pinch of salt
Butter for skillet
½ cup sliced almonds
Fresh fruit such as peaches and berries, to serve
Powdered sugar, to serve
½ cup vanilla yogurt

In a medium bowl, whisk together eggs, half & half, ⅓ cup of
Amaretto, honey and salt. Soak bread slices in egg mixture for
5-10 minutes to thoroughly saturate. Melt butter in skillet or
griddle. Place egg soaked slices in skillet and cook over medium
heat. Gently press a sprinkle of almond slices into the uncooked
side of the bread. As the bottom of the bread browns, add a little
more butter to skillet and turn over the French toast. Cook, almond-
side-down, until bread has browned and almonds are toasted.

Remove French toast from griddle and place on plate, almond-
side-up. Dust with powdered sugar if desired and top with fresh
fruit, a dollop of Amaretto flavored yogurt and a sprig of mint.
Serve with raspberry or maple syrup.

For Amaretto yogurt: Mix 1 teaspoon of Amaretto with ½ cup of
vanilla yogurt.

Arbor Guest House

This beautiful old colonial Napa Valley Inn was built in the summer of 1906. The Arbor Guest House and its spacious grounds became a bed & breakfast in 1983. Each of the five luxurious guest rooms is equipped with queen beds, period furnishings, private baths, chocolates and flowers.

Begin your day with the inn's hearty three-course breakfast. The inn's convenient location is perfect for guests who wish to see the sites. You can tour local wineries, enjoy award-winning local cuisine and browse the eclectic variety of local shops.

INNKEEPERS: Beverly & Susan Clare
ADDRESS: 1436 G. Street, Napa, California 94559
TELEPHONE: (707) 252-8144; (866) 627-2262
E-MAIL: sales@arborguesthouse.com
WEBSITE: www.arborguesthouse.com
ROOMS: 5 Rooms; Private baths
CHILDREN: Welcome
PETS: Not allowed; Resident pet

Blackberry Pecan French Toast

Makes 8 Servings

1 large loaf French bread
8 Eggs
3 cups whole milk
½ teaspoon freshly grated nutmeg
1 teaspoon vanilla extract
1 cup brown sugar, divided
2 cups blackberries (about 12 ounces)
4 tablespoons plus 1 teaspoon butter, divided
1/4 teaspoon salt
1 cup pecan halves

SYRUP:
2 cups blackberries
1 cup maple syrup
1 tablespoon fresh lemon juice

Grease a 9x13-inch baking dish. Cut bread into 1-inch slices and arrange in one layer in the bottom of the baking dish. In a large bowl, whisk together eggs, milk, nutmeg, vanilla extract and ¾ cup brown sugar. Pour mixture evenly over bread. Cover and refrigerate at least 8 hours.

Preheat oven to 350°F. Sprinkle blackberries evenly over bread mixture. Put 4 tablespoons butter in a saucepan; add ¼ cup brown sugar and salt. Stir until butter is melted. Drizzle butter mixture over bread and bake 20 minutes, or until liquid from blackberries is bubbling. In the last few minutes of baking, top French toast with toasted pecans. Be careful not to allow nuts to burn.

For the syrup: In a small saucepan, cook 2 cups blackberries and maple syrup over moderate heat until berries have burst. Pour syrup through a sieve into a heatproof pitcher. Stir in lemon juice.

KALEIDOSCOPE
INN & GARDENS

The lovingly restored Victorian Kaleidoscope Inn & Gardens is the place to stay in Nipoma. Built in 1887 from first cut redwood, the Kaleidoscope Inn takes its name from the "kaleidoscope" effect of sunlight streaming in through the stained glass bordered windows. Bask in the relaxing and welcoming atmosphere and let the proprietors of the Kaleidoscope Inn help you plan the perfect vacation!

"What a pleasure to discover a beautiful mansion just off the highway in an unknown area o us. A super shower, a lovely restful bed and a charming hostess who prepared a very sumptuous breakfast for us. We look forward to returning to this "moment in history." —Guest

INNKEEPER: Carolayne Holley

ADDRESS: 130 East Dana Street, Nipomo, California 93444

TELEPHONE: (805) 929-5444; (866) 504-5444

E-MAIL: info@kaleidoscopeinn.com

WEBSITE: www.kaleidoscopeinn.com

ROOMS: 4 Rooms; 2 Suites; Private baths

CHILDREN: Welcome

PETS: Welcome

Kaleidoscope's Baked Blueberry French Toast

Makes 6 Servings

1 24-inch baguette (old south
  dough French bread…
  include the crusts)
6 large eggs
3 cups whole milk
½ teaspoon freshly grated nutmeg
1 teaspoon vanilla extract
1/3 cup packed brown sugar
1 teaspoon unsalted butter
¼ teaspoon salt
1½ cups pecans
  (or hazelnuts or walnuts)

SUGAR TOPPING:
¼ cup brown sugar
½ stick butter
1 teaspoon vanilla extract
Cinnamon (optional)

BLUEBERRY SYRUP:
1 cup blueberries (about 6-ounces)
½ cup pure maple syrup
1 tablespoon fresh lemon juice

Liberally butter a 13x9-inch baking dish. Cut 20 1-inch slices from the baguette and arrange in one layer over bottom of baking dish. In a large bowl, whisk together eggs, milk, nutmeg, vanilla extract and brown sugar; pour mixture evenly over bread. Cover and chill dish until all liquid is absorbed by the bread, at least 8 hours, or up to 1 day.

Preheat oven to 350°F. In a shallow baking pan, spread pecans evenly and toast in oven until fragrant, about 8 minutes. Sprinkle pecans and blueberries evenly over French toast mixture. Do not turn off oven.

Over low heat, melt ½ stick of butter and mix with ¼ cup of brown sugar; stir until butter is melted. Drizzle butter mixture over bread. Bake French toast in preheated oven 20 minutes, or until liquid is bubbling. Increase temperature to 400°F and watch to make sure sugar/butter mixture has caramelized before removing from oven. Cut into squares and serve with syrup of choice.

For blueberry syrup: Cook blueberries, lemon juice and maple syrup in a small saucepan over medium heat until berries have burst, about 3 minutes. You can strain out blueberries or leave them in. Reheat syrup to serve.

Shooting Star B&B

Escape to the Shooting Star Bed & Breakfast on the magnificent North Shore of Lake Tahoe. Revel in the natural beauty of Carnelian Bay, then retire to the warmth and comfort of the inn's casually elegant rooms. Wake to the exceptional food and the endless possibilities of a day in Lake Tahoe – skiing, biking, boating, golfing, fishing – whatever suits your soul!

Savor a delicious breakfast on your own time and at your own pace. The inn offers homemade fare from original recipes, such as banana bread pancakes and eggs Lulu, full-roasted coffee and fresh fruit and juice.

INNKEEPER:	Bill Matte
ADDRESS:	315 Olive Street, Carnelian Bay, California 96140
TELEPHONE:	(530) 546-8903; (888) 985-7827
E-MAIL:	innkeeper@shootingstarbandb.com
WEBSITE:	www.shootingstarbandb.com
ROOMS:	3 Rooms; Private baths
CHILDREN:	Cannot accommodate
PETS:	Not allowed

Peachy Wheat Pancakes

Makes 8 Servings

*"For a hearty breakfast the Shooting Star way, serve these pancakes
with warm maple syrup, bacon, scrambled or over-medium eggs,
fresh seasonal fruit and plenty of orange juice!"*

— INNKEEPER, *Shooting Star Bed & Breakfast*

1 cup unbleached white flour
½ cup wheat flour
3 tablespoons sugar
1¾ teaspoons baking powder
1 teaspoon salt
2 teaspoons cinnamon
2 tablespoons unsalted butter, melted
1½ cups milk
1 teaspoon vanilla extract
2 eggs, separated
½ cup finely diced peaches, with juice

Preheat griddle; griddle is ready when a drop of water dances on
the surface. In a very large mixing bowl, combine all dry ingredients. In a medium bowl, combine milk, egg yolks, vanilla extract
and melted butter. Gently mix into dry ingredients. Add peaches
and their juice to the batter. In a separate bowl, whip the egg
whites until they are fluffy, then gently fold into batter.

Spoon batter by ¼-cupsful onto the heated griddle. When bubbles
begin to appear on the surface of the pancake, flip it over and cook
until golden brown. Top with sliced bananas and whipped cream.

CASE RANCH INN

The Case Ranch Inn is a peaceful respite in a quiet country location, where guests rave about the unparalleled hospitality and graciousness of the hosts. Enjoy antique shopping at Sebastopol and Healdsburg, hike in beautiful Armstrong Woods State Park, taste award-winning wines at nearby Sonoma County wineries or visit the magnificent coastline where the Russian River meets the sea.

In the evening, enjoy the warm surrounding of the large parlor with its fireplace and comfortable wicker furniture.

INNKEEPERS:	Diana Van Ry & Allan Tilton
ADDRESS:	7446 Poplar Drive, Forestville, California 95436
TELEPHONE:	(707) 887-8711
E-MAIL:	info@caseranchinn.com
WEBSITE:	www.caseranchinn.com
ROOMS:	3 Rooms; 1 Cottage; Private baths
CHILDREN:	Children age 10 and older welcome
PETS:	Not allowed

Lemon Oat Bran Pancakes

Makes 6 Servings

*"You can easily turn these into blueberry lemon oat bran pancakes
by simply stirring one cup of blueberries into the batter."*
— INNKEEPER, *Case Ranch Inn*

1½ cups all-purpose flour
½ cup oat bran
1 tablespoon sugar
2 teaspoons baking powder
1 teaspoon baking soda
½ teaspoon salt, or to taste
2 large eggs
3 tablespoons butter, melted, or vegetable oil
2 tablespoons lemon juice
2 teaspoons grated lemon zest
1¾ cups milk
1 cup blueberries (optional)

In a large bowl, combine flour, oat bran, sugar, baking powder,
baking soda and salt. In a medium bowl, beat eggs. Mix butter,
lemon juice and lemon zest into eggs. Mix in milk. Add egg mixture to flour mixture; stir until fairly smooth. Stir in blueberries,
if desired. Let batter stand for 5 minutes.

Heat a skillet or griddle over medium-high heat until a drop of
water dances across surface of pan before evaporating (if you are
not using a non-stick skillet or griddle, brush surface lightly with
butter or oil). Add batter by ¼-cupsful to skillet. Cook pancakes
until golden brown on each side.

TEN INVERNESS WAY

Ten Inverness Way Bed & Breakfast is located off the breathtaking Marin Coast in the heart of Point Reyes National Seashore, steps from Tomales Bay and near the towns of Olema, Inverness Park and Point Reyes. The 1904 Craftsman inn is surrounded by lush gardens, filled with the aroma of home baking and appointed with the finest décor.

"We have found a cottage home-away-from-home in the sleepy, lush,
waterfront village of Inverness. Curl up in the main room in front
of the stone fireplace and settle in for a weekend of serenity."
—San Francisco Examiner

INNKEEPER:	Teri Mattson
ADDRESS:	10 Inverness Way, Inverness, California 94937
TELEPHONE:	(415) 669-1648
E-MAIL:	inn@teninvernessway.com
WEBSITE:	www.teninvernessway.com
ROOMS:	4 Rooms; 1 Suite; Private baths
CHILDREN:	Children age 12 and older welcome
PETS:	Not allowed

Banana Buttermilk Pancakes

Makes 8 Servings

*"We serve these pancakes with
chicken-apple sausage and maple syrup."*
— INNKEEPER, *Ten Inverness Way*

4 eggs
2 cups all-purpose flour
2 cups whole-wheat flour
4 cups buttermilk
½ cup vegetable oil
¼ cup sugar
4 teaspoons baking powder
2 teaspoons baking soda
2 teaspoons salt
1 teaspoon nutmeg
4 ripe bananas, mashed
Orange slices, for garnish
Mint sprigs, for garnish
Powdered sugar, for garnish
Butter, for serving
Maple syrup, for serving

In a large bowl, beat together all ingredients, except garnish and serving ingredients, until smooth and fluffy (the more air in the batter, the lighter the pancakes). Pour batter by ¼-cupsful onto a preheated, greased griddle or skillet. Cook until lightly browned on both sides. Garnish with orange slices and a mint sprig. Dust with powdered sugar. Serve with butter and maple syrup.

INN ON RANDOLPH

Relax in the luxurious accommodations offered at Napa's Inn on Randolph. Tranquility, comfort and Southern hospitality are just a few things this inn is known for. Guests can stay in one of the "Four Seasons" rooms, comfortable cottage suites or rent an entire cottage just for themselves. Each stay includes morning breakfast and afternoon snack baskets. If you're looking for something extra, the inn offers a variety of specialty packages that include items such as wine, chocolates and even in-room couples massages.

Located in Napa's historic downtown, the Inn on Randolph is just minutes away from shops, restaurants, wine merchants and tasting bars, COPIA, the wine train and Napa's Opera House.

INNKEEPER: Deborah Coffee

ADDRESS: 411 Randolph Street, Napa, California 94559

TELEPHONE: (707) 257-2886

E-MAIL: innonrandolph@aol.com

WEBSITE: www.innonrandolph.com

ROOMS: 5 Rooms; 4 Suites; 1 Cottage; Private baths

CHILDREN: Welcome

PETS: Not allowed; Resident pet

Applesauce Blintz Pancakes

Makes 8-10 Servings

"Although I typically try to make everything 'from scratch,' the added ingredients allow for this recipe to begin with packaged pancake mix."

—INNKEEPER, *Inn on Randolph*

1 cup pancake mix
1 egg
¼ cup cottage cheese
1 cup milk
1 tablespoon vegetable oil
¼ cup sour cream
   (plus some for topping)
Optional – dash of cinnamon,
   nutmeg and/or cloves
1 cup applesauce

Place pancake mix in a medium bowl. In a separate medium bowl, whisk together egg, cottage cheese, milk, oil and sour cream. Add any optional ingredients such as cinnamon, nutmeg or cloves at this point. Stir wet ingredients into the pancake mix just until moist – do not overmix! Pour the batter on a hot griddle – try to make the pancakes larger and thinner rather than thick. Cook on one side until bubble appear then flip and cook until done. Before serving, spoon 1 tablespoon of applesauce on half of the pancake; fold in half and top with sour cream. I usually serve at least 3 pancakes per person. You can also sprinkle cinnamon and powdered sugar on top if you like.

ALBERT SHAFSKY HOUSE

 Albert Shafsky House, a beautifully restored Queen Anne Victorian located in the heart of historic Placerville, offers guests a lodging experience beyond the ordinary. Each of the three guest rooms is outfitted with its own luxurious private bath and comes complete with comfortable robes and slippers. Fresh artisan cheeses and local El Dorado County wines greet you upon arrival and a delectable homemade breakfast made from the best local ingredients awaits you every morning.

"Thanks again for a great time. My job puts me up in 4 star hotels sometimes, so my bar is pretty high. I have never received such attention and quality, even at double the price. Will recommend you to anyone traveling anywhere close to your area. As far as the friendships gained, no price can be put on that."
—Guest

INNKEEPERS:	Rita Timewell & Stephanie Carlson
ADDRESS:	2942 Coloma St., Placerville, California 95667
TELEPHONE:	(530) 642-2776
E-MAIL:	Stay@shafsky.com
WEBSITE:	www.shafsky.com
ROOMS:	2 Rooms; 1 Suite; Private baths
CHILDREN:	Cannot accommodate
PETS:	Not allowed; Resident pet

Baked Pancakes with Apple Topping

Makes 6 Servings

"This recipe started out with the apples baked in the pancake but as the years went on, they ended up in the top with a drizzle of maple syrup, whipped cream, and sometimes chopped nuts. It has been a popular dish. In fact, we have a couple who ask for it each time they visit. He says she can't make it like I do and she agrees!"

—INNKEEPER, *Albert Shafsky House Bed & Breakfast*

1½ chopped cooking apples
2 tablespoons butter
2 tablespoons cinnamon/sugar mixture
6 eggs
2 teaspoons vanilla extract
1 cup milk
1 cup flour
Sliced strawberries, to serve
Whipped cream, to serve
4 tablespoons chopped nuts, to serve
¼ cup maple syrup, to serve

Preheat oven to 400°F. While oven is heating, whisk eggs, vanilla extract and milk together in a medium bowl. Add flour and whisk for 30 seconds. Mixture will be lumpy. Spray 6 individual oval ramekins with non-stick cooking spray. Divide mixture evenly among the ramekins. Bake 20 minutes.

While pancakes are baking, melt butter in a medium skillet, chop apples (leave skin on) and place them in the melted butter. Add cinnamon/sugar mixture to apples and stir until the apples are the consistency of an apple pie mixture.

Heat maple syrup in the microwave for 30 seconds.

Place pancakes on individual plates, divide the apple mixture among the pancakes and drizzle with syrup. Garnish with sliced strawberries, whipped cream and a sprinkle of nuts. Serve immediately with sausage or home fries.

McCaffrey House Inn

The McCaffrey House Bed & Breakfast Inn is an AAA Four-Diamond inn nestled in a quiet forest hollow in the California mountains, where majestic oak, cedar and pine trees mark the edge of the Stanislaus National Forest and Emigrant Wilderness. A delightfully warm and charming country home in the California Gold Country, the inn was designed and built by innkeepers Michael and Stephanie McCaffrey.

Each morning, a full breakfast is served in the dining room. A delightful picnic lunch is available for guests with a taste for the simple pleasures in life.

INNKEEPERS:	Michael & Stephanie McCaffrey
ADDRESS:	23251 Highway 108, Twain Harte, California 95383
TELEPHONE:	(209) 586-0757; (888) 586-0757
E-MAIL:	Stephanie@mccaffreyhouse.com
WEBSITE:	www.mccaffreyhouse.com
ROOMS:	7 Rooms; 1 Suite; Private baths
CHILDREN:	Children age 6 months and older welcome
PETS:	Not allowed; Resident pets

Apple Cranberry Puffed Pancakes

Makes 6 Servings

8 eggs
1½ cups milk
1 cup flour
6 tablespoons granulated sugar
1 teaspoon vanilla extract
Pinch of salt
½ teaspoon cinnamon
¼ pound butter
3 Granny Smith apples –
    peeled and shredded*
30 fresh cranberries – smashed
3 tablespoons brown sugar
Powdered sugar
Maple syrup

Preheat oven to 425°F. In a blender, mix eggs, milk, flour, granulated sugar, vanilla extract, salt and cinnamon. Divide butter into 6 1-cup ramekins. Divide the apples and cranberries evenly among the ramekins. Place ramekins in the oven and bake until butter sizzles and the fruit is cooked soft. Remove from oven and smash cranberries with a fork; mix butter, apples and cranberries together. Pour ½-¾ of batter over the fruit. Sprinkle with brown sugar and return to oven; bake 20-30 minutes.

Remove baked pancakes from oven, sprinkle with powdered sugar and serve immediately. Offer warm syrup to top off pancakes.

Note: To save time, you can use applesauce and whole cranberry sauce in place of fresh fruit. Reduce sugar to 3 tablespoons to compensate.

INN AT THE PINNACLES

L ocated on a private vineyard estate in the Gabilan Mountains of Monterey County is a vacation retreat like no other. The Inn at the Pinnacles is a luxurious and serene sanctuary in Steinbeck Country. Just four miles from Pinnacles National Monument, guests are minutes away from bird watching, hiking and rock climbing. Monterey, Carmel and the famous local wineries are just a short drive away.

"As I breathe this fresh air, the sun warms my face.
A slight morning dew provides moisture to thirsty lands.
The harvest is near, the fragrance speaking of a new beginning.
Silence provides peace to my soul."
—Guest

INNKEEPERS:	Jan & John Brosseau
ADDRESS:	32025 Stonewall Canyon Road, Soledad, California 93960
TELEPHONE:	(831) 678-2400
E-MAIL:	info@innatthepinnacles.com
WEBSITE:	www.innatthepinnacles.com
ROOMS:	6 Suites; Private baths
CHILDREN:	Children age 3 months and older are welcome
PETS:	Not allowed; Resident pet

Apple Puff Pancakes

Makes 4-6 Servings

"This recipe was adapted from
The Old Red Inn in North Conway, New Hampshire. "
—INNKEEPER, *Inn at the Pinnacles*

3 medium-large Fuji apples,
   peeled, cored and sliced
Lemon juice
4 tablespoons butter
$2/3$ cup flour
6 eggs
1 cup milk
½ teaspoon cinnamon
¼ cup dark brown sugar
Powdered sugar, to serve

Preheat oven to 425°F. Toss apples with lemon juice. In a medium saucepan, sauté apples in melted butter until they are soft. Grease a 9x13-inch baking dish with butter or margarine and layer your apples in the bottom. In a medium bowl, beat eggs. Add flour, salt and milk to beaten egg mixture and mix well. Pour pancake mixture over apples. In a small bowl, combine brown sugar and cinnamon; sprinkle over batter. Bake 20 minutes until puffed and golden. Drizzle additional lemon juice over top of pancakes and sprinkle with powdered sugar just before serving.

Serve with maple syrup.

CLIFF CREST INN

Cliff Crest Bed & Breakfast Inn is a beautiful Queen Anne Victorian originally built in 1887. This ornate inn sits on Beach Hill overlooking the Santa Cruz Beach Boardwalk. Fine dining, beaches and shopping are all just a walk away or, if romance and relaxation are what you seek, each of the inn's elegant five guest rooms is outfitted with private baths and fireplaces.

Breakfast is served daily in the solarium dining room. Enjoy a mouthwatering meal while taking in the wonderful view of the inn's redwood shaded garden, designed by John McLaren, the man behind the Golden Gate Park in San Francisco.

INNKEEPERS: Adriana Gehriger Gil & Constantin Gehriger

ADDRESS: 407 Cliff Street, Santa Cruz, California 95060

TELEPHONE: (831) 427-2609; (831) 252-1057

E-MAIL: innkpr@cliffcrestinn.com

WEBSITE: www.cliffcrestinn.com

ROOMS: 5 Rooms; 1 Suite; Private baths

CHILDREN: Welcome

PETS: Not allowed

Adriana's Apple Torte

Makes 4 to 6 Servings

Oil or butter for greasing a 9-inch pan
2-4 medium apples, cut into 1-inch slices
1 cup Krusteaz Light & Fluffy
    Buttermilk Pancake mix, or mix of choice
¼ cup sugar
1 tablespoons olive oil
½ cup milk or half & half
4 eggs

No preheating required. Generously grease a 9-inch baking pan. Arrange cut apples over the bottom of the greased pan. In a medium bowl, combine pancake mix, sugar, olive oil, milk and eggs; whisk until smooth (consistency of pancake batter). Pour batter over apples in the baking pan. Bake at 350°F for about 35 minutes, until torte is golden brown or a toothpick inserted in the center comes away clean.

Serve with maple syrup or your favorite jam/jelly. Depending on the season, you can also add other fruits to complement the apples such as blackberries, grapes, cherries, etc.

THE INN ON FIRST

Let owners Jim and Jamie treat you to a truly memorable vacation experience at Napa Valley's Inn on First. Jim, a professionally trained chef will delight your palate daily with his high quality, organic menu offerings and Jamie promises to make your stay both welcoming and satisfying. Relax and indulge in the inn's offered spa services, or treat yourself to one of the inn's signature snack or picnic baskets.

The Inn on First will help you plan the perfect romantic getaway. Just check out their specialty packages that include discounts on hot-air ballooning, the Napa Valley Wine Train and local winery tours. The Inn is also just walking distance from downtown Napa.

INNKEEPERS:	Jim Gunther & Jamie Cherry
ADDRESS:	1938 First Street, Napa, California 94559
TELEPHONE:	(707) 253-1331; (866) 253-1331
E-MAIL:	innkeeper@theinnonfirst.com
WEBSITE:	www.theinnonfirst.com
ROOMS:	5 Rooms; 5 Suites; Private baths
CHILDREN:	Children age 12 and older welcome
PETS:	Dogs allowed; Resident pet

PB&J Pancakes

Makes ten 7-8-inch pancakes

*"We developed this recipe for some families
with children who visited the inn."*

—INNKEEPER, *The Inn on First*

4½ cups flour
4 teaspoons baking soda
2 teaspoons salt
¾ cup peanut butter
4 cups milk
4 eggs
1 tablespoon lemon juice
2 cups jam or jelly of choice
1 cup whipping cream
1 teaspoon sugar

In a medium bowl, combine flour, baking soda and salt. Melt your peanut butter in a skillet or the microwave; combine with milk in a large bowl. Add eggs and lemon juice to peanut butter mixture. Combine wet ingredients with your flour mixture. You can add more milk to make a thinner pancake if desired. Pour batter by ¼-cupsful into preheated, buttered, skillet or griddle. Cook until pancakes are lightly brown on either side. Top with whipped cream; drizzle jam on top!

For jam syrup: Heat jam – add a little water to thin out the syrup consistency.

For whipped cream: In a medium bowl, whip cream and sugar to stiff peak.

Variation: Drop chocolate chips into poured pancake batter. Replace jam with Hershey's Chocolate Sauce.

MacCallum House
Inn & Restaurant

Come and enjoy the warmth and hospitality of the MacCallum House Inn, Mendocino's finest restaurant, bar and country inn. This circa 1882 Victorian mansion was built my William Kelley was a wedding gift to his daughter, Daisy MacCallum. Filled with charm, romance and antiques, the historic landmark MacCallum House stands at the very heart of the quiet village of Mendocino.

The MacCallum House provides an extraordinary breakfast experience. Relax with the morning paper in the formal dining rooms next to the wood burning fireplaces, then, dine in the ocean-view café or, weather permitting, outside on the wraparound sun porch.

INNKEEPERS:	Jed & Megan Ayres & Noah Sheppard
ADDRESS:	45020 Albion Street, Mendocino, California 9560
TELEPHONE:	(707) 937-0289; (800) 609-0492
E-MAIL:	info@maccallumhouse.com
WEBSITE:	www.maccallumhouse.com
ROOMS:	21 Rooms; 5 Suites; 9 Cottages; Private baths
CHILDREN:	Welcome
PETS:	Welcome; Call ahead

Mendocino Wild Huckleberry Whole Wheat Pancakes with Pine Nut Butter

Makes 6 Servings

1 cup organic whole wheat flour
½ cup whole wheat pastry flour
¼ cup toasted wheat germ
¼ cup wheat bran
2½ teaspoons baking powder
1 teaspoon baking soda
½ teaspoon sea salt
¾ cup canola oil
2 cups buttermilk
2 eggs
1 tablespoon honey

½ teaspoon vanilla extract
½ cup applesauce
¾ cup huckleberries
Butter for griddle

PINE NUT BUTTER:
½ cup toasted pine nuts*
½ teaspoon sea salt
1 stick unsalted butter,
   sliced into ½-inch pieces
2 tablespoons powdered sugar

In a medium bowl, mix together wheat flour, pastry flour, wheat germ, bran, baking soda and salt. In a large bowl, mix together oil, buttermilk, eggs, honey, vanilla extract and applesauce. Combine wet and dry ingredients, stirring just until mixed (leave mixture slightly clumpy – do not overmix or pancakes will be tough). Melt butter in a heated griddle or skillet. Pour batter by ½-cupsful onto griddle; scatter 1 tablespoon of huckleberries over top. Cook until bubbles appear at the edge of the pancake. Flip over and cook until golden brown. Place two pancakes on a plate and top immediately with a ¼-inch slice of the pine nut butter. Drizzle with maple syrup. Garnish with huckleberries and a scoop of vanilla ice cream if you like.

Purée pine nuts and salt in a food processor until smooth like a creamy peanut butter. Put all of the pine nut butter ingredients into a mixer with a paddle and mix until smooth, scraping down sides as you go. It will be very soft. Place mixing bowl in the refrigerator until the mixture sets up enough to form into a log (about 15 minutes). Place butter log on parchment paper and roll into a 2-inch diameter log to store for future use.

To toast pine nuts: Preheat oven to 350°F. Place nuts in a single layer on a sheet pan and toast in oven until slightly golden (approximately 8 minutes); watch them carefully so they don't burn.

You can prepare these mixtures in advance; simply add wet ingredients to dry ingredients just before cooking.

STAHLECKER HOUSE INN & GARDENS

Secluded on one and a half acres of lush, manicured lawns and flowering gardens, the Stahlecker House Bed & Breakfast is a nostalgic gem in Napa Valley. Built in the late 1940s on the ground of an apple orchard, the property now houses the beautifully decorated inn of vintage racecar driver and pilot Ron and local artists and wife Ethel Stahlecker.

Sip fresh made lemonade on the sun deck or unwind in front of two fireplaces in the gathering rooms on a cool night. There are fireplaces in each bedroom and homemade cookies to satisfy any guest's sweet tooth.

INNKEEPERS: Ron & Ethel Stahlecker

ADDRESS: 1042 Easum Drive, Napa, California 94558

TELEPHONE: (707) 257-1588; (800) 799-1588

E-MAIL: stahlbnb@aol.com

WEBSITE: www.stahleckerhouse.com

ROOMS: 4 Rooms; 1 Suite; Private baths

CHILDREN: Welcome

PETS: Not allowed

German Pancakes

Makes 1 Serving

²/₃ cup Krusteaz pan cake mix
¾ cup water
2 tablespoons wine of choice

In a medium bowl, mix all ingredients and let stand for 5 minutes. You will need to add about ¼ cup of additional water to the batter to reach desired consistency – not too runny, not too thick. Spray a large skillet with non-stick cooking spray and heat over lowest stove setting. Put ½ of the batter in the skillet and spread over the entire surface of the pan. Cook until pancake is almost done on the top. Using a spatula, lift the edge of the pancake and flip with your fingers. Cook other side about 3 minutes. Place on a warm plate and spread with melted butter. Sprinkle powdered sugar over top and garnish with fresh lemon slices to serve.

"Breakfast like an emperor,

lunch like a king,

and dine like a beggar."

—POPULAR GERMAN SAYING

Casa Laguna Inn & Spa

Terraced on a hillside in Laguna Beach, amid tropical gardens and flower-splashed patios, the Casa Laguna Inn exudes the ambiance of bygone days when Laguna Beach was developing its reputation as an artists' colony and hideaway for Hollywood film stars.

Two lovely beaches are a few minutes walk from the inn. Located just over a mile from Main Beach, the inn is also a short distance from the many boutiques, pottery shops and galleries for which the area is famous.

INNKEEPERS: Paul Blank & François Leclair

ADDRESS: 2510 South Coast Highway, Laguna Beach, California 92651

TELEPHONE: (949) 494-2996; (800) 233-0449

E-MAIL: innkeeper@casalaguna.com

WEBSITE: www.casalaguna.com

ROOMS: 16 Rooms; 5 Suites; 1 Cottage; Private baths

CHILDREN: Welcome

PETS: Welcome

Pumpkin Ginger Waffles

Makes 8 Waffles

"This recipe is exclusive to the late fall/harvest season. We serve this flavorful waffle with real maple syrup and pecan syrup."

—INNKEEPER, *Casa Laguna Inn & Spa*

4½ cups all-purpose flour
1½ cups cornstarch
3 teaspoons baking powder
1½ teaspoons baking soda
3 teaspoons salt
4 cups milk
2 cups buttermilk
2 cups vegetable oil
6 eggs
9 teaspoons sugar
4½ teaspoons vanilla extract
2 cups canned pumpkin
2 tablespoons candied ginger

In a medium bowl, combine the flour cornstarch, baking powder, baking soda and salt; mix well. Add the milk, buttermilk, vegetable oil, eggs, sugar, vanilla extract, pumpkin and candied ginger. Mix until fully combined. Let batter stand 30 minutes.

Preheat a waffle iron. Do not use non-stick spray, the oil n the batter will allow the waffle to release easily. Follow the directions on your waffle iron to cook the waffles. Serve immediately with fruit garnish, butter and syrup with pecans.

CARTER HOUSE INNS

The Carter House Inns, an enclave of four magnificent Victorians perched alongside Humboldt Bay in Old Town Eureka, is consistently ranked as one of Northern California's top inns. Luxurious accommodations and sumptuous dining at the inn's Restaurant 301 (also considered among Northern California's best) set an indulgent tone for a getaway.

The innkeepers' passion for using only the freshest produce led them to start their own organic gardens. Today, the Carter House maintains the most extensive kitchen gardens of any inn on the West Coast.

INNKEEPERS: Mark & Christi Carter
ADDRESS: 301 L Street, Eureka, California 95501
TELEPHONE: (707) 444-8062; (800) 404-1390
E-MAIL: reserve@carterhouse.com
WEBSITE: www.carterhouse.com
ROOMS: 22 Rooms; 8 Suites; 2 Cottages; Private baths
CHILDREN: Welcome
PETS: Not allowed

Fresh Corn Waffles with Cilantro Butter

Makes 3 to 4 Servings

"Like no other waffles you have had before."
—INNKEEPER, *Carter House Inns*

1 cup all-purpose flour
½ cup yellow cornmeal
2 tablespoons sugar
2 teaspoons baking powder
¼ teaspoon salt
1 large egg
2 tablespoons unsalted butter, melted and cooled
½ cup water
1 cup fresh corn
1 teaspoon vanilla extract
Maple syrup for serving

CILANTRO BUTTER:
½ stick unsalted butter, softened
¼ cup chopped cilantro

In a large bowl, combine flour, cornmeal, sugar, baking powder and salt. In a medium bowl, whisk together egg, butter, water, corn and vanilla. Add egg mixture to flour mixture; mix until just combined. Bake waffles on a preheated, greased or non-stick waffle iron until golden. Top each waffle with cilantro butter and serve with maple syrup.

For the cilantro butter: Whisk together butter and cilantro until smooth and creamy.

Sequoia View B&B

Visitors to Sequoia View Winery enjoy a wonderful 20-acre vineyard, farm and winery near the north entrance of King's Canyon and Sequoia National Parks. This romantic bed & breakfast offers expansive views of vineyards and mountains by day and stargazing at night.

Each morning, enjoy a full country breakfast with homemade breads and jams, and fresh orange juice from the inn's trees. The winery tasting room offers handcrafted Merlots, Zinfandels and Cabernet Sauvignons, as well as the inn's own rare and unique Rhone-style Alicante Bouschet.

INNKEEPERS: Jim & Debbie Van Haun

ADDRESS: 1384 Frankwood Avenue, Sanger, California 93657

TELEPHONE: (559) 787-9412; (866) 738-6420

E-MAIL: info@svbnb.com

WEBSITE: www.svbnb.com

ROOMS: 3 Suites; Private baths

CHILDREN: Welcome

PETS: Not allowed; Resident pet

Goat Cheese Filled Crêpes with Alicante Bouschet Jelly

Makes 4 Servings

"Guests who need a gluten/wheat free and/or dairy free breakfast love these crêpes. Other guests won't even notice the alternative ingredients!"

—INNKEEPER, *Sequoia View Bed & Breakfast*

CRÊPES:
1 cup gluten free flour*
1 tablespoon oil
3 eggs
1 cup rice milk*
1 teaspoon vanilla extract
Additional oil for crêpe pan.

4 ounces goat cheese, at room temperature
Alicante Bouschet or other grape jelly,
    at room temperature

Mix crêpe ingredients together. Heat a nonstick griddle or crêpe pan and coat very lightly with oil (use a brush). Pour about 5 tablespoons of batter onto the griddle. Cook about one minute; flip and cook the other side. Continue until all batter is used (will make 12 crêpes). At serving time, spread goat cheese onto the crepes. You can either roll the crêpe or fold into thirds. Top with jelly and serve.

*If gluten and dairy are not a concern, you can use white flour and regular milk.

Egg Dishes & Breakfast Entrées

Egg Dishes & Breakfast Entrées

"*Egg dishes have a kind of elegance, a freshness, an allure, which sets them quite apart from any other kind of food, so that it becomes a great pleasure to be able to cook them properly and to serve them in just the right condition.*"

—ELIZABETH DAVID

SEVEN GABLES INN

Completed in 1886, the Seven Gables Inn is one of a parade of showy Victorians built along the oceanfront of the Monterey Peninsula. Today, guests can gaze out beveled windows at an unobstructed view of the Monterey Bay and the coastal mountains beyond.

Colorful gardens surround the inn, and guests will encounter a profusion of blooming flowers year-round. Breakfast, a lavish and elegant affair, is served in the main dining room. The lovely ritual of afternoon tea features delicious, homemade treats and imported cakes.

INNKEEPERS: Ed Flatley & Susan Flatley Wheelwright

ADDRESS: 555 Ocean View Boulevard, Pacific Grove, California 93950

TELEPHONE: (831) 372-4341

E-MAIL: None available

WEBSITE: www.pginns.com

ROOMS: 14 Rooms; 1 Suite; 3 Cottages; Private rooms

CHILDREN: Children age 12 and older welcome

PETS: Not allowed

Asparagus with Poached Eggs & Pancetta

Makes 8 Servings

"This was inspired by a traditional Italian recipe.
It works beautifully as an elegant breakfast dish."

—INNKEEPER, *Seven Gables Inn*

LIME BEURRE BLANC SAUCE
1 shallot, minced
2 tablespoons seasoned rice wine vinegar
½ teaspoon ground coriander
½ teaspoon sugar
½ cup white wine or Champagne
Juice and zest of 1 lime
2 tablespoons butter, cut into 3 pieces
Salt & white pepper, to taste

ASPARAGUS WITH POACHED EGGS
2 bunches asparagus, ends trimmed
8 large eggs, poached soft
6 slices pancetta, cut into matchstick strips
½ cup shaved Parmesan cheese
Freshly ground pepper, to taste
Freshly ground nutmeg, to taste

For the sauce: Heat a heavy skillet over medium heat. Combine shallots, vinegar, coriander and sugar; add to skillet. Add wine and cook, whisking occasionally, until shallots are very tender and liquid is reduced by half. Whisk in lime juice and zest. Add butter, 1 piece at a time, whisking well after each addition until combined. Season with salt and white pepper.

For the asparagus and poached eggs: Preheat oven to 400°F. Put asparagus in a baking dish. Scatter pancetta over asparagus. Bake until asparagus is just tender and pancetta has begun to crisp. Remove from oven and divide among plates. Top with poached egg. Sprinkle with Parmesan cheese. Drizzle with buerre blanc sauce. Season with pepper and nutmeg.

CHURCHILL MANOR

Churchill Manor is a magnificent, three-story, circa 1889 mansion listed on the National Register of Historic Places. Encompassing nearly 10,000-square feet, it is reputed to be the largest home of its time built in Napa Valley. This storybook mansion is the legacy of businessman Edward S. Churchill, one of Napa's founders.

The mansion rests amid a private acre of mature trees, lush gardens, colorful tree roses, verdant, manicure lawns and a formal fountain. An expansive veranda surrounds three sides of this elegant mansion.

INNKEEPERS: Joanna Guidotti & Brian Jensen

ADDRESS: 485 Brown Street, Napa, California 94559

TELEPHONE: (707) 253-7733; (800) 799-7733

E-MAIL: be@churchillmanor.com

WEBSITE: www.churchillmanor.com

ROOMS: 10 Rooms; Private baths

CHILDREN: Children age 12 and older welcome

PETS: Not allowed; Resident pet

Poached Eggs on Polenta with Tomato Salsa

Makes 10 Servings

"Not having an electric broiler, we could not toast English muffins to our liking ... so this is our solution, polenta instead of English muffins and salsa instead of Hollandaise sauce."

—INNKEEPER, *Churchill Manor Bed & Breakfast*

2 cups polenta
8 cups chicken stock
4 cups shredded Monterey Jack cheese
20 slices of Canadian bacon
20 poached eggs*
Salt and pepper

TOMATO SALSA
5 large ripe tomatoes, chopped
2 green onions, chopped
2 garlic cloves, minced
½ cup chopped parsley
1 chipotle pepper in Adobo sauce, chopped

For polenta: Boil chicken stock and stir in polenta. Cook and stir at reduced heat for 10 minutes. Pour polenta mixture into a ½-inch sheet pan (the pan should be filled to the top). Sprinkle Monterey Jack cheese over the polenta; cover and refrigerate until set.

Remove polenta from the refrigerator and cut into serving size wedges. Place wedges into a buttered sauté pan, cover and heat until cheese melts. In a medium sauce pan, mix together salsa ingredients and heat over medium-low heat.

To assemble: Place two polenta wedges on each plate. Top each wedge with a slice of Canadian bacon, one poached egg and hot tomato salsa.

For poached eggs: See page 125.

GERSTLE PARK INN

The Gerstle Park Inn is a quiet and secluded inn that offers absolute luxury and relaxation. Guests can enjoy private decks and patios, down comforters and fine linens. Some suites include Jacuzzi tubs, and the cottages come with a full kitchen. Take a leisurely walk amongst Gerstle Park's grand oak and redwood trees or watch deer graze in the garden while you relax and enjoy a glass of iced tea. For those interested in seeing the sights, San Francisco, Berkeley and California's Wine Country are just minutes away.

A full breakfast is served daily and early risers can enjoy a lighter, early breakfast if they choose. Complementary wine and snacks are served fireside each evening in the inn's gathering room.

INNKEEPERS: Jim & Judy Dowling, Judy Ablove

ADDRESS: 34 Grove Street, San Rafael, California 94901

TELEPHONE: (415) 721-7611; (800) 726-7611

E-MAIL: innkeeper@gerstleparkinn.com

WEBSITE: www.gerstleparkinn.com

ROOMS: 8 Suites; 4 Cottages; Private baths

CHILDREN: Welcome

PETS: Dogs allowed

California Poachies

Makes 1 Serving

2-3 sliced mushrooms, depending on size
2 tablespoons sliced zucchini
2 tablespoons chopped red bell pepper
1 tablespoon chopped red onion
2 tablespoons grated Parmesan cheese
2 eggs, poached (see below)
1 English muffin, toasted
2 slices avocado

Sauté mushrooms, zucchini, red bell pepper and red onion in butter with a little olive oil; season with salt and pepper. Place one poached egg on each half of the toasted English muffin and cover with a sprinkling of Parmesan cheese. Top each poached egg with sautéed vegetables and avocado.

To poach eggs: In a large sauce pan, heat 3-4 cups of water until almost boiling. Add 1 tablespoon of vinegar to the water (vinegar helps the egg to maintain its shape). Crack each egg into a small dish and slide the individual egg into the water. You should be able to cook about 4 eggs at a time. Keep water just below a boil, reducing heat as needed, and cook until egg whites are set but centers are still soft.

Inn at Occidental of Sonoma Wine Country

Each room and suite at the Inn at Occidental is distinctly different. Select the one that sparks your imagination and discover a treasure trove of whimsical folk art, family heirlooms and rare antique-shop finds. All rooms feature overstuffed down beds, comfortable sitting areas and fireplaces. Most rooms offer spa tubs for two, and many have private decks.

Beautifully prepared and presented, each day's fare is a feast for the eyes and the palate. Executive chef Jan Messersmith creates marvelous dishes with herbs from the inn's gardens and produce from the best Sonoma farms.

INNKEEPERS:	Jerry & Tina Wolsborn
ADDRESS:	3657 Church Street, Occidental, California 95465
TELEPHONE:	(707) 874-1047; (800) 522-6324
E-MAIL:	innkeeper@innatoccidental.com
WEBSITE:	www.innatoccidental.com
ROOMS:	15 Rooms; 3 Suites; 1 Cottage; Private baths
CHILDREN:	Children age 12 and older welcome
PETS:	Small dogs allowed; Call ahead

Occidental Eggs Benedict

Makes 8 Servings

NO-FAIL HOLLANDAISE SAUCE
24 ounces whole butter
9 egg yolks
$1/3$ cup warm water
¼ cup lemon juice
Cayenne pepper to taste
1 teaspoon sea salt
¼ teaspoon white pepper

POTATO PANCAKES
1¾ pounds Yukon gold potatoes, peeled and grated
1 small onion, grated
1 egg, beaten
2 tablespoons breadcrumbs
1 teaspoon salt
Pepper to taste
2 ounce white vinegar
1 tablespoon sea salt
16 eggs
16 slices Canadian bacon

For the hollandaise sauce: Melt the butter in a microwave-safe bowl until hot. Combine all hollandaise ingredients, except butter, together in a blender; blend 5 seconds. Slowly add butter while the blender is running. Keep the sauce warm in the top half of a double boiler over very hot water.

For the potato pancakes: Squeeze as much water from the grated potatoes as possible. Combine all the ingredients together in a medium bowl. In a hot skillet over medium-high heat, fry small rounds of potato mixture in canola oil until brown.

To poach eggs: Add vinegar to 1 quart of water. Add sea salt and heat until just under a boil. Add eggs, one at a time to water. Remove with a slotted spoon when eggs are done to preference.

To assemble, place 2 potato pancakes on a plate. Top with warm Canadian bacon and eggs. Cover eggs with hollandaise sauce and garnish with chopped parsley.

THE MARTINE INN

R anked as one of the "Top Eight B&Bs in Historic Homes" by *Bon Appétit,* The Martine Inn is an elegant getaway for the discerning traveler. With soft robes, fresh fruit in silver baskets, an acclaimed restaurant with an extensive wine and champagne list and delightful rose gardens across the grounds, guests are sure to enjoy a luxurious stay.

From the dining room, look directly out at the waves crashing against the rocky coastline of Pacific Grove on Monterey Bay. On clear days, Mt. Madonna is visible 50 miles across the bay.

INNKEEPERS: Don Martine

ADDRESS: 255 Ocean View Boulevard, Pacific Grove, California 93950

TELEPHONE: (831) 373-3388; (800) 852-5588

E-MAIL: don@martineinn.com

WEBSITE: www.martineinn.com

ROOMS: 24 Rooms; Private baths

CHILDREN: Not encouraged

PETS: Not allowed

Castroville Eggs

Makes 8 Servings

"Castroville, California is known as the 'Artichoke Capital of the World.' Marilyn Monroe was crowned Miss California Artichoke Queen in Castroville in 1947."

—INNKEEPER, *Martine Inn*

SAUCE
4 cups cream or half & half
½ teaspoon salt
¼ teaspoon white pepper
¼ cup chopped green onions
¼ cup diced pimentos
2 teaspoons cornstarch diluted
    with 2 teaspoons water

1½ cups shredded cheese of choice,
    a white cheese is recommended
2½ cups chopped artichoke hearts,
    water-packed not marinated
4 English muffins, split and toasted
8 eggs
Hot water for poaching eggs
Splash of vinegar

For sauce: Mix together all sauce ingredients in the top pan of a double boiler. Heat through and add cheese. Continue to heat until cheese has melted and add artichoke hearts.

To serve: Poach eggs in water with a splash of vinegar to keep eggs from spreading. Place one egg on each half of English muffin. Ladle warm sauce over eggs. Garnish with edible flower, parsley or paprika.

WHITE SWAN INN

With crackling fireplaces in all 26 guestrooms and suites, the White Swan Inn is a romantic, small hotel in the Nob Hill/ Union Square area of San Francisco. The inn is a visually stunning tribute to the intimate hotels of London, with dark wood paneling, rich carpets, comfortable furniture and enchanting English art.

Guests enjoy a lavish, gourmet breakfast buffet and evening wine and hors d'oevres served fireside in the cozy parlor.

INNKEEPER:	Pam Flank
ADDRESS:	845 Bush Street, San Francisco, California 94108
TELEPHONE:	(415) 775-1755; (800) 999-9570
E-MAIL:	whiteswan@jdvhospitality.com
WEBSITE:	www.whiteswanninnsf.com
ROOMS:	26 Rooms; Private baths
CHILDREN:	Welcome
PETS:	Not allowed

Mushroom Quiche

Makes 6 to 8 Servings

"This has been our most popular breakfast item for over 20 years."

—INNKEEPER, *White Swan Inn*

1 tablespoon butter
½ pound mushrooms, sliced
½ medium onion, chopped
1 cup grated Swiss cheese
½ cup grated Parmesan cheese
½ teaspoon thyme
½ teaspoon oregano
8 large eggs
2 cups milk
1 cup heavy cream
Salt and pepper, to taste

Preheat oven to 375°F. Melt butter in a skillet over medium heat. Add mushrooms and onions; cook until soft. Spread ½ of Swiss cheese and ½ of Parmesan cheese in bottom of a greased quiche or pie pan. Top with mushroom mixture. Sprinkle with remaining Swiss and Parmesan cheese. Sprinkle with thyme and oregano.

Whisk together eggs, milk, cream, salt and pepper; pour over ingredients in pan. Bake for 35-45 minutes, until set and golden brown.

APPLE BLOSSOM INN

The award winning Apple Blossom Inn Bed & Breakfast sits on 5.5 acres near Yosemite National Park. The expansive grounds include an organic apple orchard, garden and spa. Privacy is key at the Apple Blossom Inn and rooms are arranged so that each guest will feel as if they have the entire house to themselves. Each cottage style room is comfortably decorated and features its own private bath and luxury linens, perfect for a peaceful night's rest in a quiet country atmosphere.

Gourmet "Candy Apple Breakfasts" are served daily in the dining room or, weather permitting, on the deck. Guest favorites include Apple Blossom Pancakes, Candy Apple French Toast and Banana Blossom Waffles with Apple Cider Sausages. All breakfasts are Candy Arthur originals and include fresh local fruits, juices, coffee, tea, milk yogurt, cereal and breakfast breads.

INNKEEPER:	Candy Arthur
ADDRESS:	44606 Silver Spur Trail, Ahwahnee, California 93601
TELEPHONE:	(559) 642-2001; (888) 687-4281
E-MAIL:	appleblossominn@sti.net
WEBSITE:	www.appleblossombb.com
ROOMS:	3 Rooms; 1 Suite; Private & shared baths
CHILDREN:	Welcome
PETS:	Dogs & cats welcome; Resident pets

Cheesy Apple Blossom Quiche

Makes 6 Servings

2 apples, diced
½ stick butter
1 partially baked 10" pie shell
1 cup grated cheddar cheese
3 eggs
2 egg yolks
½ cup cottage cheese
1½ cups half & half
¼ teaspoon cinnamon
1 teaspoon sugar
Dash of salt

Preheat oven to 375°F. In a medium skillet, sauté apples and butter for 5 minutes. Layer apples in the bottom of the partially baked pie shell; top with cheddar cheese. In a medium bowl, beat together eggs, egg yolks, cottage cheese and half & half. Pour mixture over apples and cheese. Combine the sugar, cinnamon and salt and sprinkle over the top of the egg mixture. Bake in oven for 30-45 minutes or until firm.

HOWARD CREEK RANCH

This historic Howard Creek Ranch is a 60-acre beachfront farm bordered by miles of beaches, mountains and coastline. The inn with its expansive property offers guests on-site hiking and horseback riding on the beach or in the mountains. Guests also have access to hot tubs, a sauna and a masseuse for a little help relaxing after all that excitement. Local activities include whale watching, deep-sea fishing, white-water rafting and, of course, local wine tours.

A hearty ranch breakfast is included with your stay and the menu changes daily. If you want to stay in and relax, the ranch has plenty more to offer. You can sunbathe on the beach while you read a book from Sally's collection, use one of the barbecues and have a picnic and enjoy a beach side sunset.

INNKEEPER:	Sally Grigg
ADDRESS:	40501 North Highway One, Westport, California 95488
TELEPHONE:	(707) 964-1603
E-MAIL:	howardcreekranch@mcn.org
WEBSITE:	www.howardcreekranch.com
ROOMS:	7 Rooms; 2 Suites; 3 Cottages; Private and shared baths
CHILDREN:	Ages 10 and older welcome
PETS:	Welcome; Call ahead; Resident pets

Mitzi's Quiche

Makes 8 Servings

1 unbaked 9-inch pie shell
4 eggs
1 cup heavy cream
¼ teaspoon sea salt
¼ teaspoon fresh ground pepper
¼ teaspoon nutmeg
¼ pound fresh baby spinach
½ pound white button mushrooms,
    lightly sautéed in butter
½ cup green onions, finely chopped
1 cup grated Swiss and Cheddar cheese mix

Preheat oven to 350°F. In a medium bowl, beat eggs, salt, pepper and nutmeg; fold in cream. Place spinach, mushrooms and green onion in the bottom of the pie shell; pour egg mixture over the top. Sprinkle with cheese and baked for 45 minutes, or until eggs are set.

The Grateful Bed

This prominent, circa 1905 Victorian home was lovingly restored in 1998. The innkeepers, purveyors of nostalgic comfort, have furnished the inn with lovely antiques, quality beds and timeless treasures. The inn, located in the tree-lined Avenues of Chico, offers richly appointed bedchambers with fine linens and luxurious baths.

The inn is just a stone's throw from California State University, Bidwell Mansion State Historic Park and downtown Chico's numerous shops and restaurants.

INNKEEPERS: Rick & Carol Turner

ADDRESS: 1462 Arcadian Avenue, Chico, California 95926

TELEPHONE: (530) 342-2464

E-MAIL: thegratefulbed@sbcglobal.net

WEBSITE: www.thegratefulbed.net

ROOMS: 4 Rooms; Private baths

CHILDREN: Children age 12 and older welcome

PETS: Not allowed; Resident pets

Spinach-Artichoke-Feta Frittata with Potato Crust

Makes 4-5 Servings

'This is a winning combination of flavors.
The recipe was adapted from www.foodfit.com.'

—INNKEEPER, *The Grateful Bed*

3 tablespoons olive oil
2 potatoes, sliced thin
1 cup frozen chopped spinach
1 cup canned artichoke hearts,
    drained and chopped
¾ cup crumbled Feta cheese
4 eggs
1½ cups milk
¼ teaspoon nutmeg
¼ teaspoon salt
¼ teaspoon black pepper

Preheat oven to 325°F. Heat olive oil in a 10-inch non-stick, oven safe skillet. Layer the potato slices in an overlapping circular style over the bottom and sides of the skillet. Cook the potatoes until they begin to brown. Remove from heat and sprinkle evenly with spinach, artichoke hearts and feta cheese. In a medium bowl, mix together eggs, milk and spices; pour over the vegetables. Place the skillet in the preheated oven and bake 45 minutes. Let the frittata stand for 10 minutes. Cut into 4-5 wedges and serve.

BEN MADDOX HOUSE B&B

Built in 1876, the Ben Maddox House Bed & Breakfast sits on one acre surrounded by century old trees, a small citrus orchard, aromatic rose gardens and its own herb gardens. Much of the home, including the dining room, parlor and bedrooms, is still in its original state. Fourteen-foot ceilings, original hardwood floors and antiques grace most of the bedrooms. Ben Maddox house is conveniently located in historic Visalia, just five blocks from downtown Main Street's specialty shops and restaurants.

Breakfast is served each morning and guests can choose to dine on the deck or at private tables in the house's dining room.

INNKEEPER: Lucy Robinson-DeLucia

ADDRESS: 601 North Encina Street. Visalia, California 93291

TELEPHONE: (559) 739-0721; (800) 401-9800

E-MAIL: innkeeper@benmaddoxhouse.com

WEBSITE: www.benmaddoxhouse.com

ROOMS: 5 Suites, 1 Cottage; Private baths

CHILDREN: Children age 6 and older welcome

PETS: Pets welcome; Resident pets

Papa Joie's Frittata

Makes 4 Servings

*"My husband's grandmother made this recipe when
she came over from Italy and Papa Joie passed it on to us."*
—INNKEEPER, *The Ben Maddox House*

6 large eggs
½ ounce of half & half
½ cup red bell pepper, chopped fine
½ cup green bell pepper, chopped fine
⅓ cup red onion, chopped fine
½ teaspoon finely chopped garlic
Handful of frozen spinach*
½ ounce cheddar cheese, finely grated

Preheat oven to 400°F. In a blender or food processor, mix together eggs and half & half; set aside. In a small skillet, sauté red and green bell peppers, onion, garlic and spinach with a little extra virgin olive oil. Spoon vegetables evenly into an oven safe ramekin or pan. Add the grated cheddar cheese to the egg mixture and pour over the vegetables. Bake in preheated oven for 10 minutes. Reduce oven temperature to 375°F and bake for an additional 20 minutes, or until frittata is rising and lightly browned.

*If using creamed spinach you will need to add a little bit of butter.

OLD THYME INN

Spend enchanted nights in this ideal setting, where time seems to stand still and romance flourishes like fresh hydrangeas. The Old Thyme Inn will wash away your concerns with the everyday and transport you to an elegant world of easy sophistication and charmed relaxation.

Each of the seven guest rooms takes its name from the inn's garden. All are uniquely decorated with lovely antiques, sumptuous beds with crisp cotton linens, original fine art, Essential Elements spa amenities and fresh flowers.

INNKEEPERS:	Kathy & Rick Ellis
ADDRESS:	779 Main Street, Half Moon Bay, California 94019
TELEPHONE:	(650) 726-1616; (800) 720-4277
E-MAIL:	innkeeper@oldthymeinn.com
WEBSITE:	www.oldthymeinn.com
ROOMS:	7 Rooms; Private baths
CHILDREN:	Welcome
PETS:	No allowed; Resident pet

Artichoke Frittata

Makes 6 Servings

"A healthy and delicious breakfast entrée.
Serve with toast and chicken-apple sausage."
—INNKEEPER, *Old Thyme Inn*

1-2 tablespoons olive oil
4 green onions, finely chopped
2 medium potatoes, diced
1 medium tomato, chopped
1 (14-ounce) can artichoke hearts, quartered
2 tablespoons chopped parsley
Salt and pepper, to taste
¼ cup Pecorino Romano cheese
8 large eggs
½ cup half & half
1 cup grated Monterey Jack cheese
Sour cream, for garnish
Fresh herbs (such as basil, lemon thyme
    or rosemary) for garnish

Preheat oven to 350°F. Spray a 9-inch pie pan with non-stick cooking spray. Heat olive oil in a skillet over medium heat. Add green onions, artichoke hearts and parsley. Add potatoes; cook until golden. Add tomatoes, artichoke hearts and parsley; cook for 2 minutes. Season with salt and pepper. Spread tomato mixture in pie pan. Sprinkle with Romano cheese.

Whisk together eggs and half & half. Season with salt and pepper. Pour egg mixture over ingredients in pie pan. Sprinkle with Monterey Jack cheese. Bake for 30 minutes. Cut frittata into 6 wedges. Garnish with a dab of sour cream and fresh herbs to serve.

DUNBAR HOUSE, 1880

The Dunbar House, 1880 is a historic bed & breakfast inn that offers fine accommodations, gracious hospitality and unforgettable cuisine for travelers headed to California's historic Gold Rush Country. The inn is located in a lush garden setting and offers nearby golf, skiing, restaurants, shopping and world-class wine tasting.

"From the moment you cross the threshold if this country refuge, you will be indulged with old-fashioned hospitality and romance."
—Best Places to Stay in California

INNKEEPERS:	Barbara & Bob Costa
ADDRESS:	271 Jones Street, Murphys, California 95247
TELEPHONE:	(209) 728-2897; (800) 692-6006
E-MAIL:	innkeep@dunbarhouse.com
WEBSITE:	www.dunbarhouse.com
ROOMS:	3 Rooms; 2 Suites; Private baths
CHILDREN:	Children age 10 and older welcome
PETS:	Not allowed

Cherry Tomato & Ricotta Omelets in Toast Cups

Makes 6 Servings

"I adapted this recipe from one I found in Cooking *magazine."*

—INNKEEPER, *Dunbar House, 1880*

½ stick unsalted butter, divided
6 slices country white bread,
    cut into 5x3 ¼-inch rectangles
36 small mixed red and orange cherry tomatoes
    (about ¾ pound)
12 large eggs
½ cup milk or water
Coarse salt and freshly ground pepper, to taste
²/₃ cup ricotta cheese
2 ounces mixed green and red oak leaf lettuce
Olive oil
2 tablespoons chopped chives

Preheat oven to 425°F. Melt 2 tablespoons of butter. Brush melted butter over both sides of each piece of bread. Gently press 1 piece of bread into each of 6 muffin cups, allowing bread to overlap cup slightly. Bake bread until golden, about 10 minutes. Remove from oven and set aside.

Melt remaining 2 tablespoons of butter in a 12-inch skillet over medium heat. Add tomatoes and cook just until soft, about 3 minutes. Whisk together eggs, milk, salt and pepper until light and fluffy, about 2 minutes. Add egg mixture to tomatoes and cook for 3-5 minutes, until eggs begin to set. Lift edge of omelet with spatula and let uncooked eggs flow underneath. Continue cooking until eggs are almost set. Gently spread ricotta cheese over half of omelet. Fold omelet over and remove from heat.

Put handfuls of greens and 1 toast cup on each plate. Divide omelet among toast cups. Drizzle olive oil over greens and omelet. Sprinkle with coarse salt and pepper. Garnish with chopped chives to serve.

BIRMINGHAM B&B

The Birmingham Bed & Breakfast invites you to take a step back in time, into an era of grace, elegance and beauty. This circa 1915 historic landmark is a perfect representation of early 20th century "Prairie School" architecture. Located in the heart of Sonoma Wine Country, the Birmingham sits on two acres of fruit and nut trees, berry patches, vegetable and flower gardens. Inside, this welcoming bed & breakfast is simply decorated with fine antiques and craftsman style furniture.

Each morning guests at the Birmingham will enjoy a scrumptious and hearty two-course breakfast featuring the finest local produce and herbs, many of which are grown on-site. After breakfast, take a walk to one of the many local wineries.

INNKEEPERS: Nancy and Jerry Fischman
ADDRESS: 8970 Highway 12, Kenwood, California 95452
TELEPHONE: (707) 833-6398; (800) 819-1388
E-MAIL: info@birminghambb.com
WEBSITE: www.birminghambb.com
ROOMS: 3 Rooms; 1 Suite; 1 Cottage; Private baths
CHILDREN: Welcome; Call ahead
PETS: Pets welcome; Call ahead; Resident pets

Birmingham Eggs

Makes 4 Servings

*"This recipe was adapted from the Heritage Park Inn recipe
in* Breakfast in Bed California Cookbook:
The Best B and B Recipes in California *by Carol Frieberg."*

—INNKEEPER, *Birmingham Bed & Breakfast*

1 cup half & half
4 eggs
½ cup all-purpose flour
⅓ teaspoon dried basil
¼ teaspoon garlic powder
⅛ teaspoon salt
⅛ teaspoon freshly ground pepper
4 green onions, finely diced
½ cup sliced black olives
¾ cup diced ham (may be omitted)
1 cup shredded Italian cheese blend,
    preferably one with Asiago
½ cup diced tomato, for topping

In a blender, combine half & half, eggs, flour, garlic powder, salt and pepper. Blend until smooth.

Spray 4 large ramekins (1½-cup capacity) or custard cups with non-stick cooking spray. Layer green onions, black olives, ham and cheese in ramekins. Pour egg mixture into the ramekins; cover and refrigerate overnight.

The following morning: Preheat oven to 350°F. Remove ramekins from refrigerator and bake, uncovered, for 30 minutes. Top eggs with diced tomatoes and continue cooking until puffed and set. Serve immediately.

Garnish options: Diced green onion and shredded cheese.

Brannan Cottage Inn

CALISTOGA, CALIFORNIA ᔕ Est. 1860

The main building of the charming Brannan Cottage Inn was once part of the original Calistoga Hot Springs Resort built in 1860 by town founder, Samuel Brannan. The resort once featured 25 cottages, a theater, a horse track and a central dining hall. Of this luxurious resort, only three cottages remain. The unique and special Brannan Cottage Inn features a broad wrap-around porch and private courtyard surrounded by lush, ornamental gardens. With its distinctive architecture and deep-set historical significance, a stay at the Brannan Cottage Inn is sure to be a memorable one.

"My family was touched by your hospitality and we enjoyed getting to know you and the other guests. The food was wonderful and the atmosphere so warm and welcoming that we felt instantly at home. Keep up the good work you do here."

—Guest

INNKEEPERS: Doug & Judy Cook

ADDRESS: 109 Wapoo Avenue, Calistoga, California 94515

TELEPHONE: (707) 942-4200

E-MAIL: innkeeper@brannancottageinn.com

WEBSITE: www.brannancottageinn.com

ROOMS: 4 Rooms; 2 Suite; Private baths

CHILDREN: Welcome

PETS: Welcome

Baked Eggs
Over Sautéed Vegetables

Makes 10 Servings

"This is an excellent vegetarian meal. T
he dish has a very attractive and colorful appearance."

—INNKEEPER, *Brannan Cottage Inn*

Butter for cooking
1 large onion, chopped
1 large bunch broccoli, chopped
1 red bell pepper, sliced
2 large carrots, shredded
1 package mushrooms, chopped
1 bunch asparagus, chopped
1½ cups shredded cheddar cheese
10 eggs
Black pepper

Preheat oven to 350°F. Sauté onions, broccoli and red bell pepper in a skillet until cooked. Add carrots, mushrooms and asparagus and cook until tender. Sprinkle the cheese over the bottom of a greased 9x13-inch baking dish, reserving a small amount for the top. Add the drained, sautéed vegetables and sprinkle with the remaining cheese. Make 10 indentations in the vegetables and carefully crack one egg into each indentation; season with pepper. Cover dish and bake for about 25 minutes, checking frequently after 20 minutes to make sure the eggs do not overcook.

BLACK BEAR INN

Voted one of the top ten bed & breakfasts in California, the Black Bear Inn Bed & Breakfast is the perfect mountain get-away. This neo-rustic lodge features five guest rooms with private baths and gas fireplaces, and three romantic cabins each with its own private patio and kitchenette.

"What a splendid oasis you have created here in Lake Tahoe.
Your attention to detail is unmatched by any of your peers.
The beautiful flowers, grounds, interior design, furnishings, outstanding
breakfasts and superb accommodations - what more could one ask for?...
Thank you for a wonderful and memorable stay."
—GUEST

INNKEEPERS: Jerry Birdwell & Kevin Chandler
ADDRESS: 1202 Ski Run Boulevard, South Lake Tahoe, California 96150
TELEPHONE: (530) 544-4451; (877) 232-7466
E-MAIL: info@tahoeblackbear.com
WEBSITE: www.tahoeblackbear.com
ROOMS: 10 Rooms; Private and shared baths
CHILDREN: Children ages 16 and older welcome
PETS: Not allowed; Resident pets

Baked Herb Eggs

Makes 6 Servings

*"In the summertime, we cut fresh herbs
from our herb garden just prior to preparing this dish."*

—INNKEEPER, *Black Bear Inn*

9-10 thin slices of good deli ham, chopped
12 large eggs
3 tablespoons Stonewall Kitchen
   Traditional Pub Mustard
1 teaspoons minced garlic
½ cup sun-dried tomatoes, chopped
1 cup Cheddar cheese, grated
1 cup Monterey Jack cheese, grated
¼ cup Parmesan cheese, grated
½ teaspoon pepper
½ cup green onion, chopped
¼ cup fresh basil, chopped
Fresh oregano to taste
Fresh thyme to taste

Preheat oven to 350°F. Spray 6 ramekins (shallow oval-shaped
5-inch ramekins) with non-stick cooking spray. Evenly distribute
chopped ham among the ramekins. In a medium bowl, beat eggs.
Add mustard, sun-dried tomatoes, cheeses, pepper, green onion
and herbs. Stir well then spoon evenly into ramekins. Use fork to
push ingredients to the bottom of the egg mixture. Bake 30-35
minutes, until eggs are golden and set.

STERLING GARDENS
B&B

T he quiet Sterling Gardens Bed & Breakfast is located on
Kincaid Flat, the site of the Kincaid Gold Mine. This Country
English home has four beautiful guest rooms each inspired by a
different romantic locale. Guests can wander the expansive ten-acre
grounds, enjoy the fireplace and refreshment bar in the living room
or just relax in a hammock in the tree-shaded garden.

Sterling Gardens offers guests an award-winning two-course
breakfast each morning and a 6 PM "Wine Time" in the Common
Room featuring hors d'oevres and Sterling Vineyards wine.

INNKEEPERS:	**Charlotte & Carl Tucker**
ADDRESS:	**18047 Lime Kiln Road, Sonora, California 95370**
TELEPHONE:	**(209) 533-9300; (888) 533-9301**
E-MAIL:	**ctucker@mlode.com**
WEBSITE:	**www.sterlinggardens.com**
ROOMS:	**4 Rooms; 1 Suite; Private baths**
CHILDREN:	**Welcome**
PETS:	**Not allowed**

Baked Eggs with Mushrooms in Ham Crisps

Makes 6 Servings

¾ pound mushrooms
¼ cup finely chopped shallots
2 tablespoons unsalted butter
½ teaspoon salt
¼ teaspoon black pepper
2 tablespoons sour cream
1 tablespoon fresh tarragon
12 slices Black Forest or Virginia ham,
  without holes (10-ounces)
12 large eggs

In a heavy skillet over moderate heat, sauté mushrooms and shallots in butter with salt and pepper. Stir until mushrooms are tender and the liquid they give off is evaporated (about 10 minutes). Remove from heat; stir in sour cream and tarragon.

Preheat oven to 400°F. Fit one ham slice into each of 12 lightly oiled muffin cups. Ends will stick up and hang over edges of cups. Divide mushrooms among cups and crack 1 egg into each. Bake in center of oven until whites are cooked but yolks are still runny, about 15 minutes. Season eggs with salt and pepper. Using 2 spoons or small spatulas, carefully remove eggs, with ham, from muffin cups. Garnish each cup with fresh tarragon leaves and serve immediately.

PACIFIC VICTORIAN B&B

The elegant Pacific Victorian Bed & Breakfast sits amongst picturesque coastal mountains. Just walking distance from the beach, this California coast bed & breakfast is a great escape from

the daily grind. Brass beds covered in down comforters and fine linens grace each of the guest rooms. Whirlpool tubs, Victorian-style décor and private decks with partial ocean views will make you never want to leave.

Complimentary breakfast is served each morning in the dining room and features a variety of delightful items such as eggs benedict, blueberry pancakes, Belgian waffles and omelets.

INNKEEPERS:	Jeff & Lori Matthews
ADDRESS:	325 Alameda Avenue, Half Moon Bay, California 94019
TELEPHONE:	(650) 712-3900; (888) 929-0906
E-MAIL:	info@pacificvictorian.com
WEBSITE:	www.pacificvictorian.com
ROOMS:	4 Rooms; Private baths
CHILDREN:	Welcome
PETS:	Not allowed

Cheddar Cheese Omelet

Makes 1 Serving

*"We think the Havarti cheese
really makes this omelet different and tasty."*
—INNKEEPER, *Pacific Victorian Bed & Breakfast*

4 extra-large eggs
1 tablespoon butter
¼ cup creamy Havarti cheese, shredded
¼ cup sharp cheddar, shredded

Beat eggs very well in a small mixing bowl. Add a few shreds of havarti and cheddar cheese into beaten eggs. Melt butter in an omelet pan and pour in egg mixture. Cook eggs well on one side, then flip over to cook opposite side. Add cheese in the middle of eggs and fold in half. Serve on a serving plate and garnish on top with a few additional shreds of cheese.

*The egg is to cuisine
what the article is to speech.*

—ANONYMOUS

Poppy Hill B&B

Come and enjoy country comfort at Poppy Hill Bed & Breakfast. This beautifully restored, country home is situated in a quiet garden setting and is elegantly decorated with a stunning collection of American and European antiques and fine art. Guests can explore nearby Yosemite National Park, relax in the spa or just watch the birds.

"What a blessing to return for the second time
to such a place of beauty, calm, relaxation and breakfast delights!
You are a wonderful hostess – we'll be back."

—Guest

INNKEEPER: Mary Ellen Kirn

ADDRESS: 5218 Crystal Aire Drive, Mariposa, California 95338

TELEPHONE: (209) 742-6273; (800) 587-6779

E-MAIL: poppyhill@sierratel.com

WEBSITE: www.poppyhill.com

ROOMS: 4 Rooms; Private baths

CHILDREN: Children age 10 and older welcome

PETS: Not allowed

Eggs Picante

Makes 2 to 3 Servings

"This is sooo good and sooo easy!"
—INNKEEPER, *Poppy Hill Bed & Breakfast*

6 large eggs
6 heaping tablespoons plain yogurt
½ cup picante sauce
½ cup grated cheddar and/or Swiss cheese

Preheat oven to 375°F. In a blender, whip eggs and yogurt; pour into a pie pan sprayed with non-stick cooking spray. Bake for 20 minutes, until eggs are set. Spread picante sauce over eggs and sprinkle with cheese. Bake until cheese is melted, about 5 minutes.

Picante sauce was created in 1947 by Texan David Pace. Today, the company still uses the original recipe developed by Pace.

CASA TROPICANA INN

Overlooking the Pacific Ocean at the San Clemente Pier, the Casa Tropicana holds the promise of adventure, sun, sand and surf. With a five-mile stretch of sandy beaches and vast blue ocean, you will feel you are in a secluded tropical paradise. Guest rooms carry you into a tropical paradise of your choice. Each is named for and designed in the style of a different island resort, such as Key Largo, Bali Hai and Jungle Paradise.

The Out of Africa suite has a featherbed, fireplace, seven-foot Jacuzzi tub for two, dark woods, Oriental rugs and oak flooring.

INNKEEPER: Rick Anderson
ADDRESS: 610 Avenida Victoria, San Clement, California 92672
TELEPHONE: (949) 492-1234; (800) 492-1245
E-MAIL: info@casatropicana.com
WEBSITE: www.casatropicana.com
ROOMS: 9 Rooms; Private baths
CHILDREN: Welcome
PETS: Not allowed

Rick's Rancheros Tropicana Style

Makes 4 Servings

"This little number reflects our zesty style!"

—INNKEEPER, *Casa Tropicana Bed & Breakfast Inn*

SAUCE:
1 teaspoon sugar
½ teaspoon red pepper flakes
1 (16-ounce) can chopped tomatoes, drained
1 (32-ounce) can La Victoria Mild Green Enchilada Sauce
1 (12-ounce) can cooked chicken, drained
1 small can chopped Ortega Chiles, drained
1 teaspoon cumin
2-3 shakes Liquid Smoke
Handful tortilla chips, broken but not crushed

8 eggs
Cheddar jack shredded cheese blend, for serving
Sour cream, for serving
Scallions, thinly sliced, for serving
Flour tortillas

In a large pot over medium-low heat, caramelize the sugar and red pepper flakes. Add the tomatoes, enchilada sauce, chicken, chiles, cumin and liquid smoke. Simmer sauce for 30 minutes. Just prior to serving, add the chips. Fry two eggs over-easy for each serving. Plate the eggs and top with a ladle of sauce. Top with a handful of cheese, a dollop of sour cream and scallions. Serve with warm tortillas and fresh pineapple.

The sauce for this recipe freezes well and can easily be doubled or tripled.

CORNELIUS DALY INN

The Cornelius Daly Inn is an exquisite Colonial Revival circa 1905 mansion built by Cornelius Daly for his wife and their five children. The inn is located in the historic section of Eureka, a few blocks from the Pacific Ocean and a short drive to the majestic redwoods in Humboldt Redwoods State Park and Redwoods National Park.

The inn has been lovingly restored to its original elegance. Original features include four fireplaces and lovely Victorian gardens. Rooms are furnished with turn-of-the-century antiques reflecting the charm of the early 1900s.

INNKEEPERS:	Donna & Bob Gafford
ADDRESS:	1125 H Street, Eureka, California 95501
TELEPHONE:	(707) 445-3638; (800) 321-9656
E-MAIL:	innkeeper@dalyinn.com
WEBSITE:	www.dalyinn.com
ROOMS:	3 Rooms; 2 Suites; Private baths
CHILDREN:	Children age 12 and older welcome
PETS:	Not allowed

Southwestern Eggs & Chorizo Over Polenta

Makes 8 Servings

3¼ cups water
1 teaspoon salt
1 cup polenta
1 tablespoon butter or olive oil
1 cup sliced mushrooms
1 cup grated cheese
   (cheddar, pepper Jack or a mixture)
8 chorizo link sausages
   (removed from casings) or patties (optional)
1 tablespoon vinegar
Salsa, for serving
Sour cream, for serving

Bring water and salt to a boil in a saucepan. Add polenta, lower heat and simmer until polenta is very thick and coming away from the sides of the pan. Heat butter or oil in a small skillet over medium heat. Add mushrooms and cook until soft. Stir cheese and mushrooms into polenta; cook until cheese is melted and combined.

Lightly spray bottom and sides of an 8x8-inch baking pan with non-stick cooking spray. Spread polenta into an ½-inch-thick layer and set aside until polenta is set (the dish can be prepared to this point the night before, covered and refrigerated).

Preheat broiler. Cook chorizo, if desired, in a skillet over medium heat until done; drain any grease. Bring a saucepan of water and vinegar to a boil. Add eggs and poach until done. Cut polenta into 4 (4x4-inch) squares, then cut each square into 2 triangles. Broil polenta (or cook in a little butter or olive oil) until lightly browned. Put 1 polenta triangle on each plate. Top with chorizo and 1 poached egg. Top egg with salsa and a dollop of sour cream.

HANFORD HOUSE B&B

The Hanford House is a classic, ivy-covered, red brick inn filled with light, laughter, great food and personal attention. The inn's spacious rooms blend the elegance of a gracious past with present day comforts. Amenities include a rooftop sun deck overlooking ht hills and a shaded patio on which to enjoy a good book.

After a full, gourmet breakfast, you can pan for gold, visit a few of the many local wineries, browse through antique and specialty shops or tour historic Gold Rush buildings and sites.

INNKEEPERS:	Bob & Karen Tierno
ADDRESS:	61 Hanford Street, Highway 49, Sutter Creek, California 95685
TELEPHONE:	(209) 267-0747; (800) 871-5839
E-MAIL:	info@hanfordhouse.com
WEBSITE:	www.hanfordhouse.com
ROOMS:	7 Rooms; 3 Suites; Private baths
CHILDREN:	Welcome
PETS:	Not allowed; Resident pet

Tahoe Brunch Casserole

Makes 8 Servings

Plan ahead – this dish needs to be started the night before.

2-3 tablespoons butter or margarine,
   softened, plus 1 stick bitter
12 slices white bread, crusts removed
½ pound mushrooms, trimmed and sliced
2 cups thinly sliced yellow onion
Salt and pepper, to taste
1½ pounds bulk mild Italian sausage, browned
¾-1 pound cheddar cheese, grated*
5 eggs
2½ cups milk
1 tablespoon Dijon mustard
1 teaspoon dry mustard
1 teaspoon nutmeg
1 teaspoon salt
⅛ teaspoon pepper
2 tablespoons finely chopped parsley

Butter bread with 2-3 tablespoons of butter; set aside. Melt 1 stick of butter in a large skillet over medium heat. Add mushrooms and onions; cook for 5-8 minutes, until tender. Season with salt and pepper. In a 9x13-inch baking dish, layer ½ of mushroom mixture. ½ of sausage and ½ of cheese. Repeat layers.

Combine eggs, milk, Dijon and dry mustard, nutmeg, salt and pepper. Pour egg mixture over ingredients in baking dish. Cover and refrigerate overnight.

The next day, preheat oven to 350°F. Uncover baking dish and sprinkle with parsley. Bake for 1 our, or until bubbly. Serve immediately with fruit salad and crusty rolls.

*TIP: For a smoother texture, substitute ½ cheddar cheese and ½ Velveeta plus ¼ cup vermouth (optional) for the cheddar cheese.

ORCHARD HILL
COUNTRY INN

The award-winning Orchard Hill Country Inn, located in the heart of Julian's Historic District, offers accommodations of casual elegance where you can relax, unwind and savor an atmosphere designed with your comfort in mind. Orchard Hill welcomes guests with exacting service, attention to detail and the hospitality you would expect from a fine country inn. Guests will love the homey feel and unique décor found in each of the cottage and lodge rooms, or, if they are looking for something a little larger, they can rent the inn's cozy 1920's cottage, which can accommodate up to six guests.

"Sit under the star-studded sky gazing at Julian's few lights peeping through the trees. Toast the prospectors who mined this fine mountain gem and the Straubes for polishing it."

—COUNTRY INN'S MAGAZINE

INNKEEPERS:	The Straube Family
ADDRESS:	2502 Washington Street, Julian, California 92036
TELEPHONE:	(760) 765-1700; (800) 716-7242
E-MAIL:	information@orchardhill.com
WEBSITE:	www.orchardhill.com
ROOMS:	22 Rooms; Private baths
CHILDREN:	Welcome; Call ahead
PETS:	Not allowed

Hash Brown Casserole

Makes 8 Servings

3 tablespoons olive oil, divided

1 onion, chopped

1 (16-ounce) package frozen hash browns,
   thawed

12 eggs

1 cup sour cream

16 slices bacon, cooked crisp and crumbled

3 cups grated cheddar cheese

1 bunch green onions, sliced

Preheat oven to 375°F. Heat 2 tablespoons of oil in a small skillet over medium heat. Add onions and cook until soft. Spray a 7x11-inch baking dish with non-stick cooking spray. Toss hash browns with remaining 1 tablespoon of oil. Combine onions and hash browns; spread in baking dish. Bake for 30-40 minutes, until hash browns are browned.

Scramble eggs and sprinkle or spread over hash brown mixture in baking dish. Spread a thin layer of sour cream over eggs (reserve some sour cream for garnish). Sprinkle bacon, then cheese over sour cream (the dish can be prepared to this point, covered and refrigerated overnight). Bake for 30 minutes (do not overcook). Top each serving with a dollop of sour cream and some green onions.

VILLA DE VALOR-
HILDRETH HOUSE 1898

Treat your senses to a step back in time, to memories, of the turn of the century. Villa De Valor Bed & Breakfast, located in the heart of Julian, is a formal, Victorian home full of charm and elegance, known in its heyday as the most elegant home in Julian. The inn's gracious front porch is perfect for relaxing and enjoying the beautiful mountain top views. An inviting hammock awaits you on the side of the house.

Located an hour from San Diego at 4,200 feet, guests can enjoy gold mine and winery tours, shopping, carriage rides and mountain trails.

INNKEEPERS:	Valorie Ashley
ADDRESS:	2020 Third Street, Julian, California 92036
TELEPHONE:	(760) 765-3865; (877) 968-4552
E-MAIL:	stay@villadevalor.com
WEBSITE:	www.villadevalor.com
ROOMS:	3 Suites; Private baths
CHILDREN:	Children age 13 and older welcome
PETS:	Not allowed; Resident pet

Cheese Blintz Egg Soufflé

Makes 6 Servings

"My mom felt that food was too precious to practice on. Therefore, we were not allowed to cook, just watch – and I did. I watched my mom and my grandmothers cook during many hours in the kitchen. They were all great cooks and cooked by 'a bit of this' and a 'little bit of that' – no recipes. Hence, it is the way I cook today. I serve this soufflé with potatoes, a meat, homemade biscuits and fried peaches."

—INNKEEPER, *Villa de Valor Bed & Breakfast*

4 extra-large eggs
⅓ cup half & half
1 tablespoon sour cream
Salt and pepper, to taste
Lawry's Seasoned Salt, to taste
6 frozen cheese blintzes
1½ tablespoons unsalted butter
Grated Monterey Jack and mild cheddar cheese

Preheat oven to 400°F. Beat eggs well with a whisk. Add half & half and sour cream; beat well. Add several shakes of salt, pepper and Seasoned Salt; neat again – you should feel it in your wrist.

Spray a soufflé dish with non-stick cooking spray. Put blintzes in dish in a "wagon wheel" pattern. Place butter pieces between blintzes. Put a handful of each cheese between each blintz (this will keep them in place). Pour egg mixture over and between blintzes. Bake for about 40 minutes, until soufflé rises and top glows with a golden yellow, orange-ish tan. Cut soufflé into 6 wedges and serve.

Side Dishes & Sauces

Side Dishes
& Sauces

" *No man can be wise*
on an empty stomach. "

—GEORGE ELIOT

BARTELS RANCH & COUNTRY INN

Located near the heart of Napa Valley, Bartels' Vineyard Ranch and Bed & Breakfast Country Inn is tucked away from the bustle of town, yet is just six minutes from St. Helena's finest restaurants, wineries and shops. The inn's 60-acre country estate overlooks a 100-acre valley surrounded by private vineyards and breathtaking views. Guests can watch horses and deer graze in peaceful meadows from this romantic, hillside hideaway.

Bartels' inviting accommodations feature a collection of original art, floral wall coverings, Persian rug accents and warm Wine Country colors.

INNKEEPER:	Jami Bartels
ADDRESS:	1200 Conn Valley Road, St. Helena, California 94574
TELEPHONE:	(707) 963- 4001
E-MAIL:	innkeeper@bartelsranch.com
WEBSITE:	www.bartelsranch.com
ROOMS:	4 Rooms; 1 Suite; Private baths
CHILDREN:	Welcome
PETS:	Not allowed; Resident pets and bird sanctuary

Jami's Potatoes Magnifique

Makes 8 to 10 Servings

"These amazing potatoes are great for parties, breakfast or dinner.
Quick and easy to prepare, and very rich!"

—INNKEEPER, *Bartels Vineyard Ranch Bed & Breakfast Country Inn*

5 baking potatoes, boiled and sliced
  (peeled or unpeeled)
1 cup sour cream
½ (8-ounce) package cream cheese
¼ cup chopped pimentos
½ large red or Vidalia onion, thinly sliced
Curry powder, to taste
Salt and cayenne pepper, to taste
Chopped parsley, to taste
Sliced or chopped fresh basil, to taste
¾ pound sharp cheddar cheese, grated
Paprika, for garnish

Preheat oven to 350°F. In a buttered 5-quart casserole dish, layer ingredients in the following order; potatoes, sour cream, cream cheese, pimentos and onion. Lightly sprinkle with curry powder, salt, cayenne, thyme, parsley and basil. Repeat layers and seasoning until potatoes are used up. Sprinkle with cheese. Sprinkle paprika over entire casserole. Bake for 20 minutes, or until casserole is bubbly and cheese has melted.

DeHaven Valley Inn

DeHaven Valley Inn was built in 1875 as a seep and cattle ranch. The Manor House still stands, surrounded by 20 acres of flower-carpeted meadows, rolling coastal hills, a meandering creek and the Pacific Ocean. Take the inn's private trail along the crystal clear DeHaven Creek that runs through the middle of the property. You can see the creek's final exit into the Pacific Ocean as it flows underneath Highway One.

Meals at Dehaven are freshly made and many ingredients come from the inn's own garden. The inn's restaurant serves fabulous four-course dinners Wednesday through Sunday nights.

INNKEEPERS: Dave & Tammy Doriot
ADDRESS: 39247 North Highway One, Westport, California 95488
TELEPHONE: (707) 961-1660
E-MAIL: dehavenvalleyinn@wildblue.net
WEBSITE: www.dehavenvalleyinn.com
ROOMS: 5 Rooms: 2 Suites: 2 Cottages: Private & shared baths
CHILDREN: Welcome; Call ahead
PETS: Welcome; Call ahead

Potato Cake with Bacon & Blue Cheese

Makes 4 to 6 Servings

3 pounds Russet potatoes, peeled
   and cut into 1-inch cubes
2 tablespoons vegetable oil
¼ pound bacon, chopped into 1/4-inch dice
½ stick butter, melted plus
   ½ stick butter, cut into pieces
¼ cup minced shallots
1 tablespoon minced garlic
3 tablespoons minced chives
¼ pound blue cheese, crumbled
Salt and pepper, to taste

Preheat oven to 350°F. Bring a large pot of lightly salted water to a boil. Add potatoes and cook for 5-8 minutes, until about half-done. Remove from heat and drain well.

Cook bacon in a skillet over medium-high heat until lightly browned. Remove and drain on paper towels. Combine bacon, potatoes, melted butter, shallots, garlic, chives and cheese; stir gently to combine. Season with salt and pepper.

Spread bacon mixture in an oven-proof skillet, pressing down to compress mixture. Dot cut up butter around the edge of the skillet. Transfer skillet to oven and bake for about 20 minutes, until golden brown. Remove skillet from oven and let potato cake stand for 5 minutes before slicing and serving.

CHELSEA GARDEN INN

In the Chelsea Garden Inn's private, latticed courtyard, with its tree-lined garden paths and secluded swimming pool, you'll feel as if you are miles from anywhere. It is a wonderful place to watch

the seasons change. Yet, you are only two blocks from shops, restaurants, spas and wine tasting on historic Calistoga's Main Street.

The poolside social room, with its vaulted ceiling, large fireplace and wonderful library, is a favorite of inn guests. A delicious full breakfast is served each morning in the bistro-style dining room.

INNKEEPERS:	Dave & Susan DeVries, Connie McDonald & Jennie Juarez-Ornbaum
ADDRESS:	1443 Second Street, Calistoga, California 94515
TELEPHONE:	(707) 942-0948; (800) 942-1515
E-MAIL:	innkeeper@chelseagardeninn.com
WEBSITE:	www.chelseagardeninn.com
ROOMS:	1 Room; 3 Suites; 1 Cottage; Private baths
CHILDREN:	Welcome
	Not allowed

Spicy Potato Pie

Makes 12 Servings

9 eggs
¾ cup milk
$\frac{1}{8}$ cup butter, melted
¾ cup all-purpose flour
2¼ teaspoons baking powder
Dash cayenne pepper
½ teaspoon salt
1½ cups small curd cottage cheese
6 cups pepper Jack cheese
24 ounces frozen shredded hash brown potatoes,
   thawed (plain or southwestern)

Preheat oven to 350°F. In a large bowl, beat eggs, milk, and butter. Stir in flour, baking powder, cayenne pepper and salt. Add cheeses and slightly more than half of the potatoes; mix well. Spray 2 9-inch glass pie plates with non-stick cooking spray. Spread mixture evenly over bottom of the pie plates. Top with remaining potatoes. Bake 35 minutes, or until golden brown. Serve with salsa and sour cream if desired.

CAMELLIA INN

The Camellia Inn, a charming 1869 Italianate Victorian inn, is located in the heart of the Sonoma County Wind Country. More than 50 varieties of camellias bloom on the inn's landscaped grounds, surrounding the villa-style swimming pool. Interior architectural treasures include twin marble fireplaces, beautiful double parlors and inlaid hardwood floors.

Don't miss "Chocolate Covered Wednesdays," a day of chocolate decadence from morning chocolate croissants to evening chocolate truffles and port.

INNKEEPER:	Lucy Lewand
ADDRESS:	211 North Street, Healdsburg, California 95448
TELEPHONE:	(707) 433-8182; (800) 727-8182
E-MAIL:	info@camelliainn.com
WEBSITE:	www.camelliainn.com
ROOMS:	9 Rooms; 3 Suites; 1 Cottage; Private baths
CHILDREN:	Welcome
PETS:	Dogs allowed; Call ahead

Camellia Inn Sausage Pie

Makes 8 Servings

"This is Del Lewand's Scottish son-in-laws favorite recipe.
He likes it best for breakfast, lunch and dinner. It is an honor
to have his approval of this dish, as everyone knows that the pie
is a tasty little icon of the Scots' gastronomy fare."

—INNKEEPER, *Camellia Inn*

1 package skinless sausage links
3 cups frozen potatoes O'Brien
¼ cup chopped green onions
2 tablespoons milk
6 ounces cream cheese
½ cup grated cheese – any kind
Salt and pepper, to taste
Butter to spread over potatoes

BATTER
¾ cup biscuit mix
$1/_3$ cup milk
2 eggs

Preheat oven to 375°F. Grease a deep pie plate; spread in potatoes
and cheese. Pour melted butter over potatoes. In a medium bowl,
mix together onion, milk, softened cream cheese, salt and pepper.
Spread over potatoes. In a skillet, lightly brown the sausages and
arrange them, spoke fashion, over the potatoes. In a medium bowl,
beat together batter ingredients. Pour batter around the sausages
and bake 25-30 minutes, until lightly browned. Cut into 8 wedge
shaped pieces.

Tiffany House B&B

Nestled among spreading oaks, high on a hilltop with panoramic views, sits the Tiffany House, a late Victorian two-story home. A large, shaded deck with comfortable wicker furnishings, a quaint gazebo and a relaxing hammock create a sense of nostalgia and tranquility.

Bedrooms have queen-size beds covered in hand-crocheted bedspreads and embroidered pillowcases, down pillows and cozy robes. Each room has a view of the magnificent Mt. Lassen mountain range. The Oak Room's sitting area features a dozen signed Wallace Nutting originals.

INNKEEPERS: Susan & Brady Stewart

ADDRESS: 1510 Barbara Road, Redding, California 96003

TELEPHONE: (530) 244-3225

E-MAIL: tiffanyhse@aol.com

WEBSITE: www.tiffanyhousebb.com

ROOMS: 4 Rooms; 1 Cottage; Private baths

CHILDREN: Welcome

PETS: Not allowed; Resident pets

Spicy Smoked Salmon Corn Cake

Makes 2 Servings

"This is adapted from Gourmet *magazine's* Quick Kitchen Cookbook. *Our guests are surprised to have salmon for breakfast. It's one of our favorite dishes."*

—INNKEEPER, *Tiffany House Bed & Breakfast Inn*

¼ cup plus 2 tablespoons yellow cornmeal
3 tablespoons all-purpose flour
¼ teaspoon baking soda
¼ teaspoon salt
1 large egg, lightly beaten
3 tablespoons cream cheese, softened
¼ cup plus 2 tablespoons buttermilk
½ cup fresh or frozen (thawed) corn
3 tablespoons finely chopped chives
   (or 1 tablespoon dried)
9 pepperoncini peppers, drained,
   seeded and finely chopped
3 ounces finely chopped smoked salmon
   (about ⅓ cup)
Sour cream, for serving
Chopped red onion, for serving
Lemon slices, for serving

In a small bowl, whisk together cornmeal, flour, baking soda and salt. In a medium bowl, whisk together egg and cream cheese. Whisk buttermilk into egg mixture.

Coarsely chop ½ of corn; stir into egg mixture along with remaining corn, chives, pepperoncinis, smoked salmon and cornmeal mixture just until combined.

Drop batter by ¼-cupsful onto a large, non-stick or greased griddle or skillet; spread batter slightly to form 3½- to 4-inch cakes. Cook cakes for 2-3 minutes per side, until golden brown on both sides. Serve with sour cream, chopped red onion and lemon slices.

LAKE LA QUINTA INN

The unique Lake La Quinta Inn is located on a "lake in the desert." This European style bed & breakfast was built to resemble a French Chateau, the owners are Italian and the innkeeper is English! Lake La Quinta is the perfect place for pampered relaxation. Each individually themed guest room has a private patio or deck where guests can enjoy the mountain and lake views surrounding this exclusive inn.

Treat yourself to a day at the inn's spa. Services include massages, facials, reflexology and aromatherapy. Once you're fully relaxed, enjoy some of the activities the area has to offer – hot air ballooning, golf, bike riding and hiking nearby Joshua Tree National Park.

INNKEEPER: Julia Miskowicz
ADDRESS: 78-120 Caleo Bay Drive, La Quinta, California 92211
TELEPHONE: (760) 564-7332; (888) 826-4546
E-MAIL: stay@lakelaquintainn.com
WEBSITE: www.lakelaquintainn.com
ROOMS: 11 Rooms; 2 Suites; Private baths
CHILDREN: Welcome
PETS: Not allowed

Ham & Lake La Quinta Dates

Makes 4 Servings

*"This is so yummy – guests are skeptical until they taste the glaze.
We literally pick the dates from the tree outside the inn.
Can't get more local than that."*

—INNKEEPER, *Lake La Quinta Inn*

4 ounces butter
1 cup brown sugar
1 cup chopped dates
3-4 ounce fully cooked Danish ham,
    cut into 4 even portions

Melt butter in a non-stick skillet, add sugar and stir. Add dates
and sauté over low heat until golden brown. Add ham pieces and
turn until heated through. Divide ham evenly onto 4 serving
plates; drizzle with excess sauce and serve with scrambled eggs and
English muffin.

*Food is the most
primitive form of comfort.*

—SHEILA GRAHAM

SIMPSON HOUSE INN

c. 1874

Simpson House Inn

Bed & Breakfast
Santa Barbara, California

The Simpson House Inn, North America's only AAA Five-Diamond bed & breakfast inn, is secluded on an acre of English gardens, yet is only a five-minute walk from Santa Barbara's restaurants, theaters, shops and museums. Mountain hikes or beach walks, in-room spa services or relaxing in the garden – invigorating or calming – the choice is yours.

"The professional service and elegant touches
of an expensive hotel in a setting that allows you the illusion
of weekending at a friend's posh country home."
—THE LOS ANGELES TIMES

INNKEEPERS:	The Davies Family & Janis Clapoff
ADDRESS:	121 East Arellaga Street, Santa Barbara, California 93101
TELEPHONE:	(805) 963-7067; (800) 676-1280
E-MAIL:	info@simpsonhouseinn.com
WEBSITE:	www.simsonhouseinn.com
ROOMS:	8 Rooms; 4 Suites; 3 Cottages; Private baths
CHILDREN:	Welcome
PETS:	Not allowed

Macket Mushroom Strudel

Makes 4 Servings

*"This is one of our newest recipes and
it is quickly becoming a guest favorite."*

—INNKEEPER, *Simpson House Inn*

4 tablespoons butter
1 full sheet puff pastry (24x13 inches)
1 pound fresh white mushrooms, chopped
1 bunch green onions, chopped
1 cup pecans
11 ounces goat cheese
Salt and pepper
Egg wash

Preheat oven to 350°F. Heat butter in a large sauté pan until
it just starts to turn brown. Add mushrooms and green onions
and cook until mushrooms begin to brown. Add pecans and
sauté 2 minutes. Remove from heat and allow to cool about 5
minutes. Add goat cheese to mixture, stirring until cheese
is smooth. Season with salt and pepper to taste.

Cut pastry sheet in half. Place 1½ cups of the mushroom mixture
down the center of each puff pastry sheet. Fold the sheet over and
seal the ends together, lengthwise. Place on cookie sheets, seam-side-
down and brush with egg wash. Bake until pastry is brown all
over, about 25-30 minutes.

FARMHOUSE
INN & RESTAURANT

The family owned Farmhouse Inn & Restaurant sits in the heart of Sonoma County's Russian River Valley wine region. Siblings Catherine and Joe fuse simplicity and family tradition with comfort and luxury earning the inn both Top Pick Hotel and Top Pick Restaurant in Fodor's California Wine Country, 2008. Farmhouse Inn has also been a top rated restaurant in Zagat's San Francisco three years running. This magnificent inn is just minutes from wineries, canoeing and picnicking areas, shopping, ballooning and cycling. The Sonoma Coast is just 30 minutes by car, or you can bask in the relaxing atmosphere of the inn's own spa.

Named one of the "World's 36 Best Food Destinations" in 2007 by *Gourmet* Magazine, Farmhouse Inn's Chef Steve Litke prepares seasonal menus using the freshest local ingredients. Guests can enjoy menu items such as Seared Rare Nantucket Bay Scallops, Zinfandel Braised Beef Short Rib, and Seared Hudson Valley Foie Gras. Top it off with a local wine recommendation by Wine Director Jeff Kruth and you'll see that a dining experience at the Farmhouse Inn will be both sumptuous and memorable.

INNKEEPERS: Catherine & Joe Bartolomei
ADDRESS: 7871 River Road, Forestville, California 95436
TELEPHONE: (707) 887-3300; (800) 464-6642
E-MAIL: innkeep@farmhouseinn.com
WEBSITE: www.farmhouseinn.com
ROOMS: 2 Rooms; 2 Suites; 6 Cottages; Private baths
CHILDREN: Children age 12 and over welcome
PETS: Not allowed

Lacinato Kale

Makes 4 Servings

*"We serve this dish with our
Blood Orange and Star Anise Braised Pork Shank."*

—INNKEEPER, *Farmhouse Inn*

2 bunches organic lacinato kale
¼ cup olive oil
4-6 garlic cloves, peeled and sliced
2 shallots, peeled and sliced
Pinch of red chili flakes
Salt and pepper to taste

Cut kale leaf off stems and discard the stems. Cut leaves into 2-inch portions. Blanch in heavily salted water until tender. Place in ice bath to cool. When cooled, remove kale and squeeze off excess water.

In a large sauté pan, heat oil with garlic and shallot over medium-high heat until softened. Add chili flakes, salt, pepper and kale; cook until warmed through. Serve immediately.

Harkey House B&B

This elegant 1874 Victorian house was once the home of Sutter County Sheriff, William Pickney Harkey. Today, the Harkey House Bed & Breakfast boasts three exquisitely decorated guest rooms and one luxurious private cottage. Each of rooms is decorated on a different theme – The Empress Room is soothingly adorned with Asian influenced wallpaper and antiques while the Tuscan Room will make guests feel as if they are relaxing in an Italian villa. Harkey House is both family and pet friendly and is walking distance from movie theaters, local restaurants and shopping.

Each morning guests will be treated to a full gourmet breakfast that can be served in the French Country style dining room or poolside. Harkey House also offers an in-room tea and coffee selection, evening turn down service, a private spa for two and homemade cookies.

INNKEEPERS:	Bob & Lee Jones
ADDRESS:	212 C Street, Yuba City, California 95991
TELEPHONE:	(530) 674-1942
E-MAIL:	lee@harkeyhouse.com
WEBSITE:	www.harkeyhouse.com
ROOMS:	3 Rooms; 1 Cottage; Private baths
CHILDREN:	Welcome
PETS:	Pets allowed; Call ahead

Corn Soufflé

Makes 8 Servings

*"A guest shared this recipe with us years ago
and it is still a favorite with many guests. Comfort food!"*
—INNKEEPER, *Harkey House Inn*

2 eggs, slightly beaten
1 box Jiffy Corn Muffin mix
8 ounces sour cream
1 (4-ounce) stick butter, melted
1 can creamed corn
1 can Mexican niblet corn (do not drain)
½ cup diced red bell pepper, optional
¼ cup diced onion, optional

Preheat oven to 375°F. In a large bowl, combine beaten eggs, Jiffy Muffin mix, sour cream and melted butter. Mix until well combined; add creamed and Mexican niblet corn, red bell pepper and onion. Pour mixture into a greased 9x13-inch pan and 30-40 minutes.

HISTORIC SAND ROCK FARM B&B

Historic Sand Rock Farm is the perfect Santa Cruz bed & breakfast because of its ideal location just outside the city. A fusion of country inn and European retreat, the inn provides an unparalleled blend of gracious hospitality and a serene environment.

Start a relaxing day with an early morning stroll through the fields, or read the paper on the deck overlooking the beautiful gardens. A gourmet array of seasonal treats awaits, such as a warm, cinnamon-laced morning bun followed by a delicious entrée such as Golden goat cheese soufflé.

INNKEEPER: Kris Sheehan

ADDRESS: 6901 Freedom Boulevard, Aptos, California 95003

TELEPHONE: (831) 688-8005

E-MAIL: reservations@sandrockfarm.com

WEBSITE: www.sandrockfarm.com

ROOMS: 2 Rooms; 3 Suites; Private baths

CHILDREN: Welcome

PETS: Not allowed

Goat Cheese Soufflé

Makes 12 Servings

*"This soufflé is one of our most popular dishes. It is wonderful atop
a seasonal salad, such as springtime asparagus tips, English peas and
baby greens or sun-dried tomatoes and summer corn with romaine
lettuce. In fall, try caramelized onion, diced apples and butter lettuce.
In winter, try greens with balsamic vinaigrette and dried fruits."*

—INNKEEPER, *Historic Sand Rock Farm*

¼ cup dry breadcrumbs
3 tablespoons butter,
   plus extra for buttering ramekins
3 tablespoons cake flour
1 cup milk
10 ounces goat cheese, divided
3 egg yolks
Salt and pepper, to taste
1 cup egg whites (about 7 egg whites)

Preheat oven to 425°F. Butter 12 (5-ounce) ramekins or standard
muffin cups. Dust with breadcrumbs, then turn out excess breadcrumbs. Melt 3 tablespoons of butter in a saucepan over medium
heat. Whisking constantly, add flour. Whisk in milk and cook for
about 3 minutes, until mixture has thickened to the consistency
of a thin pudding.

Crumble ¾ of the goat cheese into a bowl. Pour hot milk mixture over goat cheese; mix well. Add egg yolks; mix well. Season
with salt and pepper. Beat egg whites with a mixer until stiff
peaks form. Fold ½ of egg whites into milk mixture, then fold
in remaining egg whites. Divide ½ of milk mixture among the
ramekins. Crumble remaining goat cheese into ramekins, then
top with remaining milk mixture.

Put ramekins in a large baking pan. Add enough boiling water to
baking pan to come halfway up the sides of ramekins. Bake for
25 minutes, or until golden. Remove from oven and let ramekins
stand in pan for 15 minutes. Using a towel to hold ramekins, run
a knife around the inside rim to loosen soufflés. Turn out soufflés
onto serving plate to serve.

THE GROVELAND HOTEL

F ounded in 1849, Groveland was a rough-and-ready gold mining
town at Yosemite's front door. The original adobe Groveland
Hotel at Yosemite National Park was constructed around 1850.
Known as "The Best House on the Hill" at the height of the Gold
Rush, the Groveland Hotel is the ideal base for all sorts of recreation
in the Sierra Nevada Mountains.

The Groveland Hotel features outstanding cuisine prepared with
fresh, local, seasonal ingredients. Most herbs are grown in the hotel's
garden and produce comes from local farms.

INNKEEPERS: Peggy & Grover Mosely

ADDRESS: 18767 Main Street, Groveland, California 95321

TELEPHONE: (209) 962-4000; (800) 273-3314

E-MAIL: guestservices@groveland.com

WEBSITE: www.groveland.com

ROOMS: 14 Rooms; 3 Suites; Private baths

CHILDREN: Welcome

PETS: Welcome; Resident pets

Aunt Dora's Southern Barbecue Sauce

Makes About 16 Pints

*"This recipe is from an incredible menu of Southern barbecue
as it was prepared several generations ago at Leonard's Barbecue
on Old Highway 51 South in Memphis, Tennessee. It was
passed down to me from my aunt, Dora Simmons. As a former
schoolmate and neighbor of Elvis Presley – we're all from Memphis –
we enjoyed this type of food often. We treasure this recipe today
and share it with our guests every summer."*

—INNKEEPER, *the Groveland Hotel at Yosemite National Park*

7 cups chopped onion
1 gallon ketchup
8 cups water
2 cups chili powder
¼ cup dry mustard
2½ cups Worcestershire sauce
2 teaspoons minced garlic
1 gallon red wine vinegar
4 pounds dark brown sugar
2½ cups plus 3 tablespoons paprika
12 bay leaves
2 cups crushed red pepper flakes

Combine all ingredients in a large pot. Bring just to a boil, then immediately remove from heat (mixture will be very thin). Cool and seal in sterilized containers with tight-fitting lids. Store for 30 days to age. When ready to use, open only as much as is needed. When sauce is exposed to air, it will thicken immediately. Use on pork, chicken, beef, shrimp, etc.

NOTE: You can cut this recipe down, but the results may not be the same. Be sure to follow canning safety procedures.

Appetizers, Soups & Salads

Appetizers, Soups & Salads

"Cooking is a way
of giving and
making yourself desirable."

—MICHEL BOURDIN

LAVENDER INN

Lavender Inn's sophisticated bed & breakfast was originally built in 1875 as the first schoolhouse in Ojai. Over the years it has evolved from a town recreation center to a hotel and then later remodeled as a bed & breakfast. A lavender scented English garden, majestic oaks, fountains and ponds adorn the expansive lawns and help make a stay at the Lavender Inn a truly rejuvenating experience

"Ojai's Lavender Inn, a 1874 schoolhouse-cum-boutique hotel,
will make you feel like you flew eleven hours on Air France instead
of just driving two, as will a massage in the Provence Cottage.
The Ojai Culinary School calls the inn home, so feel free to take a class
… You'll be miles away from the office, feeling totally out of this world."
—*DAILY CANDY LA*

INNKEEPERS: Erica Smith & Kathy Hartley
ADDRESS: 210 East Matilija Street, Ojai, California 93023
TELEPHONE: (805) 646-6635; (877) 646-6635
E-MAIL: innkeeper@lavenderinn.com
WEBSITE: www.lavenderinn.com
ROOMS: 7 Rooms; 1 Suite; Private & shared baths
CHILDREN: Welcome
PETS: Dogs allowed

Melted Brie with Mushrooms

Makes 8 Servings

"This hors d'oevre has been a staple at our family parties for years. Now we offer it at the Lavender Inn for Wine & Cheese Hour and for some of our special events. Guests always rave about it!"

—INNKEEPER, *Lavender Inn*

5 green onions, chopped
½ tablespoon olive oil
8 ounces sliced mushrooms
¼ cup vermouth
¼ cup soy sauce
1 small 4-5'round of brie
1 tablespoon chopped parsley or
   purple kale, optional

Preheat oven to 350°F. Sauté onions in olive oil. When the onions are getting limp, add the mushrooms. Stir in vermouth and soy sauce and remove from heat. Slice the top off the brie, but leave the sides and bottom intact and place in an oven-proof serving dish (preferably round). Pour mushroom mixture over the brie and bake for 20 minutes until the brie has melted. Garnish with parsley or kale and serve on sliced French bread or crackers.

BRIDGE CREEK INN

Nestled near the vineyards of the Edna Valley, just minutes from San Luis Obispo, the Bridge Creek Inn offers pastoral views of the Santa Lucia Mountains and a spectacular, nightly show of uncountable stars.

This custom-designed bed & breakfast sits on ten acres of gently rolling hills with a seasonal stream. Here, you can retreat from pressures of daily life by relaxing in the outdoor spa, visiting the many nearby wineries or exploring the scenic California coast.

INNKEEPERS:	Sally & Gene Kruger
ADDRESS:	5300 Righetti Road, San Luis Obispo, California 93401
TELEPHONE:	(805) 544-3003
E-MAIL:	info@bridgecreekinn.com
WEBSITE:	www.bridgecreekinn.com
ROOMS:	2 Rooms; Private baths
CHILDREN:	Cannot accommodate
PETS:	Not allowed

Brie with Strawberries in Puff Pastry

Makes 8 Servings

½ cup raspberry, strawberry or plum jam
¼ cup chopped strawberries
½ teaspoon chopped rosemary,
   plus rosemary sprigs, for garnish
1 sheet puff pastry (½ of a 17-ounce package),
   thawed
1 (13-ounce) wheel Brie cheese
   (about 6- to 7-inches in diameter)
1 egg, beaten
Grape clusters, for garnish
Baguette slices or crackers, for serving

Preheat oven to 400°F. In a small bowl, combine jam, strawberries and chopped rosemary. Roll out puff pastry slightly into a 12-inch square.

Cut rind off top of Brie. Put cheese, cut-side-up, in center of puff pastry sheet. Spread jam mixture over top of Brie. Fold puff pastry over Brie; wet edges and press to seal. Brush pastry with egg. Transfer to a baking sheet and bake for 20 minutes. Cool for 10 minutes. Garnish with rosemary sprigs and grape clusters. Serve with baguette slices or crackers.

Cypress Inn
on Miramar Beach

The Cypress Inn on Miramar Beach is an upscale bed & breakfast inn with outstanding, unobstructed ocean views and five miles of white sand beach. The goal of the inn's interior design is to bring the outdoors inside with a palette of nature's colors. Mexican folk art and hand-carved wooden animals add to the colorful celebration of nature.

The breakfast menu varies daily with fresh fruit, home baked croissants and delicious entrées such as artichoke quiche, Spanish egg sarape or the house specialty – peaches and cream French toast.

INNKEEPER:	Chris Miller
ADDRESS:	407 Mirada Road, Half Moon Bay, California 94019
TELEPHONE:	(650) 726-6002; (800) 832-3224
E-MAIL:	cypressinn@innsbythesea.com
WEBSITE:	www.cypressinn.com
ROOMS:	18 Rooms; Private baths
CHILDREN:	Welcome; Call ahead
PETS:	Not allowed

Artichoke Heart Dip

Makes 8 Servings

1 (8-ounce) jars marinated artichoke hearts
¾ cup mayonnaise
½ cup shredded Parmesan cheese
¼ cup shredded mozzarella
½ cup breadcrumbs
4 tablespoons pesto

Preheat oven to 350°F. In a medium bowl, mix together all ingredients until well combined. Reserve some of the Parmesan and bread crumbs for topping. Bake 30 minutes, or place under broiler on a low rack for 10 minutes.

Serve with crackers or sliced, toasted baguettes.

The artichoke, like the oyster,

is a food that makes

an indelible impression

on the untried tongue.

—BERT GREENE

INN AT DEPOT HILL

Located two blocks from the beach in the Mediterranean-style village of Capitola-by-the-Sea is the award-winning Inn at Depot Hill. The inn has received the prestigious Mobil Four-Star award each year since 1977 and has been named one of the top ten inns in the country.

Appointments are rich and luxurious, and echo an opulent past. The inn's upscale rooms are named for and luxuriously decorated in the style of legendary parts of the world: the Cote d'Azur Room captures the essence of a chic auberge in St. Tropez; the Portofino Room, and Italian coastal villa.

INNKEEPERS:	Claire Whitelaw
ADDRESS:	250 Monterey Avenue, Capitola, California 95010
TELEPHONE:	(831) 462-3376; (800) 572-2632
E-MAIL:	depothill@innsbythesea.com
WEBSITE:	www.innsbythesea.com
ROOMS:	12 Rooms; Private baths
CHILDREN:	Children age 8 and older welcome
PETS:	Not allowed

Asiago Cheese Dip
with Beer Bread

Makes 10 to 12 Servings

BEER BREAD

3 cups all-purpose flour

½ cup sugar

1 tablespoon honey, warmed slightly (aids mixing)

1 (12-ounce) bottle beer (amber or red ale works well)

1 cup grated cheese (cheddar works well)

1 tablespoon butter, melted

Preheat oven to 350°F. Combine flour and sugar. Add honey and beer; mix thoroughly. Stir in cheese. Place dough in a 9x5-inch loaf pan. Brush with melted butter. Bake for 1 hour. Cool, then slice.

ASIAGO CHEESE DIP

2 tablespoons butter

12 mushrooms, sliced

¼ cup chopped oil-packed sun-dried tomatoes

½ cup chopped green onions

Salt and pepper, to taste

1 cup mayonnaise

1 cup sour cream

1½ cups grated Asiago cheese, divided

Preheat oven to 350°F. Melt butter in a skillet over medium heat. Add mushrooms, sun-dried tomatoes and green onions; cook until mushrooms are soft. Season with salt and pepper. Combine mayonnaise, sour cream and 1 cup of Asiago cheese. Stir in mushroom mixture until well combined. Transfer mixture to a small baking dish. Sprinkle with remaining ½ cup Asiago cheese. Bake for 15 minutes, or until mixture is smooth and cheese topping has melted. Serve warm with beer bread.

1801 First Luxury Inn

This luxurious Napa Valley bed & breakfast inn welcomes guests to a world of casual elegance and relaxed refinement in Wine Country. 1801 First caters to your every luxurious whim. Each bath pampers you with an oversized soaking tub and spacious separate shower or Jacuzzi. Sensual bath amenities and soothing robes complete the experience.

In each room, exquisite beds are lavishly adorned with fine linens, down comforters and Egyptian cotton coverlets. Romantic fireplaces and inviting sitting areas encourage lazy, tranquil afternoons.

INNKEEPERS: Darcy & Tom Tunt

ADDRESS: 1801 First Street, Napa, California 94559

TELEPHONE: (707) 224-3939; (800) 518-0146

E-MAIL: info@1801first.com

WEBSITE: www.1801first.com

ROOMS: 5 Suites; 3 Cottages; Private baths

CHILDREN: Not able to accommodate

PETS: Not allowed

Italian Cheese Torte

Makes 8-12 Servings

"Our guests love this at our wine and appetizer hour."

—INNKEEPER, *1801 First Luxury Inn*

8 ounces softened cream cheese
2 ounces softened unsalted butter
½ cup pesto
½ cup sun-dried tomatoes, finely diced
1 teaspoon garlic powder
½ teaspoon kosher salt
½ teaspoon black pepper

In a medium bowl, whip together cream cheese and butter with an electric mixer; add garlic powder, salt and pepper and whip until light and creamy. Line a shallow bowl with plastic wrap. Spoon 3 tablespoons of pesto into the bottom of the lined bowl, then cover with ⅓ cup of the cream cheese mixture, top with a layer of sun-dried tomatoes. Continue layering ingredients in this manner until all ingredients have been used. Cover with plastic wrap and refrigerate 4 hours minimum or up to overnight.

Before serving, remove top layer of plastic wrap and turn bowl over onto a decorative platter. Serve with rustic crackers.

VAGABOND'S HOUSE INN

Vagabond's House
Carmel-By-The-Sea, California

Nestled in the heart of the village of Carmel-by-the-Sea, near Monterey Bay, Vagabond's House Inn is a charming, brick, half-timbered English Tudor country inn. A delightful experience begins as you walk up the front steps and enter an almost magical place.

Accommodations include extraordinarily charming guest rooms with fireplaces and private baths and entrances. Vagabond's House Inn has been selected as the "Best Inn on the West Coast" for three consecutive years by Arrington's Bed & Breakfast Journal.

INNKEEPER:	Julie Campbell
ADDRESS:	4th and Dolores, Carmel, California 93921
TELEPHONE:	(831) 624-7738; (800) 262-1262
E-MAIL:	innkeeper@vagabondshouseinn.com
WEBSITE:	www.vagabondshouseinn.com
ROOMS:	14 Rooms; Private baths
CHILDREN:	Children age 10 and older welcome
PETS:	Welcome

Sun-Dried Tomato Pesto Spread

Makes 6 Cups

*"This spread is great on crackers or baguettes.
It will keep in the refrigerator for a week or more."*

—INNKEEPER, *Vagabond's House Inn*

3 (8-ounce) jars oil-packed sun-dried tomatoes,
  undrained
2 (8-ounce) packages feta cheese
$\frac{1}{8}$ teaspoon garlic salt
Oregano, to taste
1 (8-ounce) package cream cheese
1 cup minced fresh parsley
$\frac{1}{3}$ cup grated Parmesan cheese
French baguette slices or crackers, for serving

Purée sun-dried tomatoes in a food processor. Crumble feta
cheese into a large bowl. Add sun-dried tomatoes, garlic salt,
oregano and cream cheese; mix well. Adjust seasonings to taste.
Add parsley and Parmesan cheese; mix well, cover and chill.
Before serving, microwave for 20-30 seconds, until spreadable.
Serve with baguette slices or crackers.

OLD WORLD INN

The historic, circa 1906 Old World Inn was originally built as a private residence. The inn has an eclectic combination of architectural styles, detailed with wood shingles, wide, shady porches, clinker brick and leaded and beveled glass windows and is furnished with painted antiques. Scandinavian colors dominate the parlor, which, along with its fireplace and soft classical music, is the perfect escape from the rushing world.

Guest rooms have been individually decorated with coordinated linens. Most have a Victorian claw-foot tub, and one has a private spa tub.

INNKEEPERS:	Russ Herschelmann & Sharon Fry
ADDRESS:	1301 Jefferson Street, Napa, California 94559
TELEPHONE:	(707) 257-0112; (800) 966-6624
E-MAIL:	innkeeper@oldworldinn.com
WEBSITE:	www.oldworldinn.com
ROOMS:	9 Rooms; 1 Cottage; Private baths
CHILDREN:	Welcome
PETS:	Not allowed

Olive Tapenade

Makes 8 to 12 Servings

*"We pair this tapenade with freshly baked bread
and pita chips as part of our wine and appetizer hour –
it is always a big hit. This recipe is adapted from one at the Ink
House Bed & Breakfast in Napa."*
—INNKEEPER, *Old World Inn*

¾ cup canned ripe black olives
1 teaspoon lemon juice
½ cup pimento-stuffed Spanish green olives
1 tablespoon capers
½ teaspoon Italian seasoning
1 teaspoon minced garlic
1½ teaspoons chopped fresh parsley
1½ tablespoons pine nuts or sunflower seeds
Dash of cayenne pepper
1 (8-ounce) package cream cheese,
    for serving
Sliced bread, pita chips and/or
    gourmet crackers for serving

Put all ingredients, except cream cheese and bread, in a food processor and pulse for 30 seconds. Chill and serve over cream cheese with sliced bread, pita chips and/or gourmet crackers.

Mount View Hotel & Spa

Escape to a place where time stands still and romance is found. Pamper yourself in our day spa, take a dip in the pool and Jacuzzi, and then fall into a serene sleep in our feather beds. Forget that anywhere else in the world exists. Welcome to the historic Mount View Hotel & Spa. Built in 1917, Mount View is among the premier historic hotels of Napa Valley. Here guests will find wooded hillsides, fine dining and luxurious spas.

Each of the inn's 32 rooms is uniquely decorated and comes with luxury amenities. Aveda bath products, feather beds, fluffy robes and fresh ground coffee can be found in each room and you can enjoy a complimentary continental breakfast delivered right to your door!

INNKEEPERS:	Andrea Trinidad
ADDRESS:	1457 Lincoln Avenue, Calistoga, California 94515
TELEPHONE:	(707) 942-6904; (800) 816-6877
E-MAIL:	info@mountviewhotel.com
WEBSITE:	www.mountviewhotel.com
ROOMS:	19 Rooms; 10 Suites; 3 Cottages; Private baths
CHILDREN:	Welcome
PETS:	Not allowed

Scrumptious Stuffed Mushrooms

Makes 6 Servings

"This was specially created by Chef Joel Ehrlich (Napa Valley)
who has graciously shared his secret recipe with us!"

—INNKEEPER, *Mount View Hotel & Spa*

2 pounds button mushrooms
½ bunch thyme
½ cup chopped bacon
½ large yellow onion, diced
2 tablespoons extra virgin olive oil
1 tablespoon chopped garlic
¼ pint heavy cream
⅓ cup Aslago cheese
¾ cup breadcrumbs
1 egg
Truffle oil, optional

Preheat oven to 400°F. De-stem mushrooms. Dice half of the mushrooms and all of the stems. In a large sauté pan, heat oil over medium heat then add bacon and cool until all the fat has been rendered out. Add the diced mushrooms and cook for 10 minutes. Add onion to skillet and sauté until they are translucent. Add the garlic and thyme and cook for 1 minute before adding cream. Reduce liquid by half and remove from heat. Add the cheese, breadcrumbs and egg to the mixture. Stuff the remaining whole mushrooms with the mixture and bake about 20 minutes until soft. Drizzle with truffle oil to serve.

LINCOLN OAKS

This 1917 Craftsman-style home is much more than a simple bed & breakfast. Lincoln Oaks is home to a three bedroom traditional bed & breakfast as well as a Wedding Garden and reception hall. Each of the guest rooms is individually themed and decorated. Guests can relax in the Tuscan style McCourtney room, the Hydrangea room, or the French Room. Whichever you choose, you'll enjoy unique antique furnishings, private baths and lush, pillow-topped mattresses.

A special morning beverage tray service is available in each of the guest rooms and a full breakfast featuring farm fresh eggs and fresh baked scones is served daily in the bed & breakfast's dining room.

INNKEEPER: Janet Moranda
ADDRESS: 2819 McCourtney Road, Lincoln, California 95648
TELEPHONE: (916) 645-1965
E-MAIL: janet@lincolnoaks.com
WEBSITE: www.lincolnoaks.com
ROOMS: 3 Rooms; Private baths
CHILDREN: Welcome; Call ahead
PETS: Not allowed

Lincoln Oaks House Pâté

Makes 8 servings

1 can beef consommé
1 tablespoon Worcestershire sauce
1 envelope gelatin
$\frac{1}{3}$ soup can of cold water
8 ounces cream cheese
8-9 ounces liverwurst
½ bunch green onions -
    chopped white part only
½ cup small button mushrooms,
    sliced small and cut into ½-inch pieces, optional*
Chopped pistachios, skins rubbed off, optional
8-9-inch ring mold with 6 cup capacity

Heat consommé with Worcestershire sauce. Soften gelatin in the cold water then add to the consommé mixture to dissolve. Pour small a small amount of the consommé into the bottom of the mold and set in the refrigerator to set (use just enough to cover the bottom of the mold). Pour the rest of the consommé into a blender. Allow to cool and then add cream cheese and liverwurst; blend completely. Stir in the green onions and any of the optional items you may be using.

Gently pour mixture over the set gelatin in ring mold. Return mold to the refrigerator and allow to set up. You can make this up to a day ahead of time. Display mold, gelatin-side-up, on a platter with crostini.

This recipe can easily be halved if you have a smaller group.

For mushrooms: If you are using the mushrooms, sauté them in butter and brandy until lightly browned before adding to the pâté mixture.

THE GOLDEN GATE HOTEL

In 1986, the Golden Gate Hotel's owners settled down to create the kind of hotel they had always dreamed of – comfortable and charming, full of flowers and serving a great cup of coffee. Morning coffee, tea, juice and croissants are served in the downstairs parlor for a civilized start to the day.

Rooms in this circa 1913, Edwardian hotel are furnished with antiques and wicker. Some of the baths still have their original claw-foot tubs. The original birdcage elevator connects the four floors. Pictures – from the historic to the absurd – line the halls, adding Old World ambiance.

INNKEEPERS: John and Renate Kenaston

ADDRESS: 775 Bush Street, San Francisco, California 94108

TELEPHONE: (415) 392-3702; (800) 835-1118

E-MAIL: info@goldengatehotel.com

WEBSITE: www.goldengatehotel.com

ROOMS: 25 Rooms; Private & shared baths

CHILDREN: Welcome

PETS: Dogs welcome; Resident pets

Chicken Soup
with Apples & Leeks

Makes 6 Servings

1 whole chicken, cut up,
   washed and patted dry
Salt and pepper, to taste
½ stick butter, divided
3 leeks
2 Granny Smith apples, peeled
   and cut into ¼-inch cubes
3 cups chicken broth
½ cup dry apple juice
3 tablespoons Calvados or
   other apple brandy
½ cup heavy cream

Season chicken with salt and pepper. Melt 2 tablespoons of butter in a soup pot over medium heat. Add chicken, skin-side-down, and cook for 8 minutes. Turn chicken and cook for 5 minutes longer. Remove chicken to a bowl and set aside.

Pour any butter or fat out of soup pot. Melt remaining 2 tablespoons of butter in soup pot over medium heat. Cut greens off leeks, leaving only about 1-inch of green. Slice leeks, add to pot and cook for 10 minutes, stirring occasionally, until soft, but not brown. Add chicken, apples, both, vinegar and apple juice to leeks. Bring mixture to a slow simmer. Skim any fat. Cover pot and simmer very gently for 15 minutes, until chicken is cooked through. Remove chicken and let cool.

Skin and debone chicken. Cut meat into ½-inch chunks. Skim any remaining fat from soup. Add Calvalos and heavy cream. Bring to a simmer and season with salt and pepper. Add chicken and simmer for 2 minutes. Serve immediately in hot bowls.

VILLA TOSCANA B&B

Guests at the Villa Toscana Bed & Breakfast will feel as if they have stepped into another world. The authentic Italian villa sits in the heart of Martin & Wyrich's estate vineyards and resembles an Italian vacation resort rather than a simple bed & breakfast. In addition to the eight villa suites, Villa Toscana has a 3,000 plus square foot Winemaker Residence available for rental. The Winemaker Residence even comes complete with its own private dining room.

A private on-site bistro, caterers, in-room spa treatments and complimentary wine and hors d'oevres are just a few of the luxurious amenities guests will enjoy at the Villa Toscana Bed & Breakfast.

INNKEEPER:	Therese Corea
ADDRESS:	4230 Buena Vista, Paso Robles, California 93446
TELEPHONE:	(805) 238-5600
E-MAIL:	myvillatoscana@martinweyrich.com
WEBSITE:	www.myvillatoscana.com
ROOMS:	8 Suites; 1 Cottage; Private baths
CHILDREN:	Welcome
PETS:	Not allowed

Toscana Corn Bisque

Makes 8 Servings

3 peeled Yukon gold potatoes, sliced thin
¼ cup butter
1 large yellow onion
8 cups heavy cream
2 cups bottled water
1 tablespoon salt
1 teaspoon white pepper
1 cup dry vermouth
6 ears whole corn (roasted in husk for 30 minutes)
Splash of Tobasco Sauce (optional)

In a large pot, cook butter and sliced potatoes for 5-7 minutes, do not brown. Add onions and cook over medium-low heat for another 5 minutes. Add cream, water and vermouth. Cook until the potatoes are tender, about 25-30 minutes. Add the remaining ingredients, reserving 1 cup of corn. Cook for 5 more minutes then purée in blender to liquefy; soup should be very smooth. Add the reserved corn. Check soup for desired thickness; add water to dilute if necessary. Season with Tobasco, to taste. Garnish with croutons or minced chives. Serve hot.

THE SPRINGVILLE INN

In 1911, the warm and inviting Springville Inn was built in Tule River Country to provide lodging, food and drink for travelers to the southern Sierras. The inn remains a treasured part of local history and has stood the test of time, watching over Springville for almost 100 years. The innkeepers have tirelessly and lovingly restored and refurbished the inn to its past glory.

Rooms and suites at the Springville Inn are filled with Western Pine furnishings, quilts and ceiling fans. A delicious continental breakfast is served to guests each day.

INNKEEPER: Carleen Hemmerling
ADDRESS: 35634 Highway 190, Springville, California 93265
TELEPHONE: (559) 539-7501; (800) 484-3466
E-MAIL: info@springvilleinn.com
WEBSITE: www.springvilleinn.com
ROOMS: 8 Rooms; 2 Suites; Private baths
CHILDREN: Children age 12 and older welcome
PETS: Not allowed

Spinach Salad with Pear Nectar Vinaigrette & Candied Walnuts

Makes 4 to 6 Servings

$^1/_3$ cup white vinegar
$^1/_3$ cup vegetable oil
$^1/_3$ cup pear nectar
1 teaspoon Dijon mustard
$^1/_4$ teaspoon salt
$^1/_8$ teaspoon pepper
12 ounces fresh baby spinach

CANDIED WALNUTS
1 cup walnuts
$^1/_2$ cup sugar
2 tablespoons butter or margarine,
   plus extra for greasing foil

In a screw-top jar, combine vinegar, oil, pear nectar, mustard, salt and pepper. Cover and shake well to mix (can be covered and refrigerated up to 1 week). Shake again before serving. Divide spinach among plates. Top with pear nectar vinaigrette. Sprinkle with candied walnuts.

For the candied walnuts: Line a baking sheet with foil; butter foil. Combine walnuts, sugar and 2 tablespoons of butter or margarine in a heavy, 10-inch skillet over medium heat. Cook, shaking skillet occasionally (do not stir), until sugar is golden brown. Remove from heat and pour nuts onto a baking sheet. Cool completely, then break into clusters.

THE QUEEN ANNE HOTEL

This one-of-a-kind San Francisco hotel began life as a finishing school for girls in the late 1800s. With your choice of forty-eight different rooms, guests are guaranteed a truly unique and comfortable experience. Each of the elegant rooms is decorated with Victorian heirloom antiques, luxury amenities and private baths.

The Queen Anne offers guests free concierge service, courtesy car service to downtown San Francisco, afternoon sherry and tea and a complimentary continental breakfast. The hotel also offers room service from many of the local eateries.

INNKEEPER:	Michael Wade
ADDRESS:	1590 Sutter Street, San Francisco, California 94109
TELEPHONE:	(415) 441-2828; (800) 227-3970
E-MAIL:	stay@queenanne.com
WEBSITE:	www.queenanne.com
ROOMS:	41 Rooms; 7 Suites; Private baths
CHILDREN:	Welcome
PETS:	Not allowed

Franklin's Grilled Eggplant Salad with Prawns

Makes 4 to 6 Servings

¼ cup raw rice
1 teaspoon olive oil
10 large prawns, cleaned and deveined
3 Japanese eggplants
1 small red onion, chopped
¼ cup tomatoes, chopped
1 tablespoon fish sauce
1 tablespoon rice wine vinegar
2 sprigs basil or mint
1 fresh lime

Brown rice in a frying pan until golden brown. Grind rice and set aside for garnish. In a small skillet, heat oil and brown the prawns over very high heat for a short time. Be careful not to overcook. Poke holes in the eggplant with the tip of a knife (to prevent them from exploding) and grill or broil until tender. Remove from heat and arrange on a large platter. Lay the prawns, onions, tomatoes and basil, or mint, over the top of the eggplant. Pour fish sauce and vinegar over the salad and sprinkle with ground rice and lime juice to serve.

BREWERY GULCH INN

The Brewery Gulch Inn, built with ancient virgin redwood timbers eco-salvaged from the Big River, sits on ten acres overlooking Smuggler's Cove. The inn, with its Craftsman-style architecture and décor, offers ocean views, fireplaces, Jacuzzi tubs, private decks, luxurious amenities, gourmet organic cuisine and comfortable, well-appointed rooms.

"From the moment we arrived to the moment we left,
we felt wonderfully cared for. The accommodations were lovely and
the food was comparable to a high-end restaurant."
—*SAN FRANCISCO CHRONICLE SUNDAY TRAVELER*

INNKEEPERS: Guy Pacurer & Jo Ann Stickle

ADDRESS: 9401 North Highway 1, Mendocino, California 95460

TELEPHONE: (707) 937-4752; (800) 578-4454

E-MAIL: innkeeper@brewerygulchinn.com

WEBSITE: www.brewerygulchinn.com

ROOMS: 10 Rooms; Private baths

CHILDREN: Children age 13 and older welcome

PETS: Not allowed

Roasted Chestnut & Gorgonzola Stuffed Mushroom Caps

Makes 30 Pieces

"The chestnuts I used in this recipe came from dry-farmed 100-year-old chestnut trees. Their nutty flavor blended well with the Gorgonzola. It was my first attempt at using chestnuts from raw product."

—CHEF, *The Brewery Gulch Inn*

30 fresh chestnuts
½ pound Gorgonzola cheese
30 medium Baby Bella mushrooms
⅛ cup plus 2 tablespoons extra virgin olive oil, divided
2 teaspoons sea salt
2 coves garlic
¼ cup chopped parsley

Preheat oven to 350°F. Roast chestnuts for 20 minutes; place in a bowl and cover with a wet towel to steam. Peel once the chestnuts have cooled. Place mushroom caps sprinkled with ⅛ cup of extra virgin olive oil and 2 teaspoons of sea salt on a sheet pan and par bake for 10 minutes. Remove and allow to cool. In a small skillet, sauté garlic in remaining 2 tablespoons olive oil. Place garlic, chestnuts, cheese and parsley in a food processor and purée for 30 seconds. Spoon mixture into the mushroom caps and bake for 10-15 minutes. Serve at room temperature.

Sesame Somen Noodles with Shiitake Mushrooms

Makes 8 to 10 Servings

*"When I worked at Louie's Backyard in Key West,
we served a similar noodle salad with peanut butter.
It was quite spice, but I prefer this milder preparation."*
—CHEF, *The Brewery Gulch Inn*

1 (12-ounce) package somen noodles
8 ounces shiitake mushrooms
½ cup plus 2 tablespoons extra virgin olive oil, divided
¼ cup toasted sesame oil
¼ cup rice wine vinegar
¼ cup shoyo or soy sauce
1 cup chopped scallions
½ cup honey
¼ cup chopped cilantro
1 tablespoon sambal paste or siracha*
¼ cup orange juice

Cook somen noodles in salted water and strain. Remove stems and cut shiitake mushrooms into strips. Sauté mushrooms in 2 tablespoons of oil for 1 minute. In a large bowl, whisk together remaining ingredients. Toss noodles and shiitake mushrooms with dressing and serve at room temperature.

*Sambal paste and siracha sauce can be found in any major grocery store on the international/Asian food aisle with other condiments.

Rainbow Beet Salad

Makes 10 to 12 Servings

"This dish has a very intense color
nd is sure to compliment any table."
—CHEF, *The Brewery Gulch Inn*

4 large red beets (about 1 pound)
4 large golden beets (about 1 pound)
¼ cup sherry wine vinegar
1 tablespoon sea salt
¼ cup walnut oil
1 cup toasted walnuts
½ teaspoon fresh ground pepper
2 teaspoons chives

Boil beets together in salted water until you can insert a paring knife in the center. Cool and peel the beets, golden beets first then the red beets – keep the cooked, peeled beets separated. Dice or cut the golden beets into wedges and place them into a large bowl; toss with vinegar, oil, salt, nuts, pepper and chives. Just prior to serving, cut or dice the red beets and add them to the mixture. Toss only once or twice as the red beets will bleed into the golden ones. Serve either cold or at room temperature.

Luncheon & Dinner Entrées

Luncheon & Dinner Entrées

It's a lovely thing —
everyone sitting down together,
sharing food.

—ALICE MAY BROCK

BALLARD INN

Located in Santa Ynez Valley about 40 minutes from Santa Barbara, the Ballard Inn offers comfortably elegant accommodations in a peaceful and quiet setting in the heart of Santa Barbara Wine Country.

Chef Budi Kazali shares his unique, globally inspired approach to cooking at the Ballard Inn's acclaimed restaurant. Chef Kazali, who has worked at such renowned restaurants as the James Beard award winning Blued Ginger in Boston and San Francisco's Gary Danko, is particularly inspired by the variety of local wines which pair so beautifully with his Pacific Rim cuisine.

INNKEEPER:	Christine Forsyth
ADDRESS:	2436 Baseline Avenue, Ballard, California 93463
TELEPHONE:	(805) 688-7770; (800) 638-2466
E-MAIL:	innkeeper@ballardinn.com
WEBSITE:	www.ballardinn.com
ROOMS:	15 Rooms; Private baths
CHILDREN:	Children age 12 and older welcome
PETS:	Not allowed

Pan-Seared Duck Breasts with Cherry Pinot Noir Sauce

Makes 4 Servings

FOR THE DUCK
4 duck breast halves (8- to 9-ounces each)
4 sprigs thyme
2 cloves garlic, chopped

FOR THE CHERRY PINOT NOIR SAUCE
3 tablespoons dried cherries
1 tablespoon raisins
3 tablespoons brandy
2 shallots, minced
2 cloves garlic, minced
1 tablespoon butter
1 cup Pinot Noir wine
¼ cup balsamic vinegar
1 cup chicken stock
1 cup beef stock
1 tablespoon butter

For the duck: Score the skin of duck in a crosshatch pattern. Trim excess fat. Rub duck with thyme and garlic. Cover and refrigerate overnight. The next day, preheat oven to 400oF. Sear duck, skin-side-down, in an oven-proof skillet over medium-high heat, until some of the fat is rendered and skin is golden brown. Turn duck and transfer skillet to oven. Roast duck for 8 minutes for medium-rare, or to desired doneness. Remove from oven and let rest for 5 minutes. Serve with cherry Pinot Noir sauce.

For the sauce: Soak cherries and raisins in brandy until plump. Strain; reserve brandy. Melt butter in a skillet over medium heat. Add garlic and shallots; cook until shallots are softened. Add cherries and raisins. Deglaze pan with reserved brandy. Reduce until nearly dry. Add wine; reduce until nearly dry. Add vinegar; reduce to syrup. Add chicken and beef stocks; reduce until sauce thickens enough to coat the back of a spoon. Stir in butter until melted and combined. Season with salt and pepper.

ARTISTS' INN

The Artist's Inn Bed & Breakfast, a circa 1895 home built in the Midwestern Victorian style, originally served as a family home as well as the base for the Johnson Egg & Poultry farm. Today, the Inn has been completely refurbished and features a variety of rooms and suites each decorated to represent a different artist or artistic period. Guests can relax on the front porch, read the paper in the parlor, or take the Gold Line to downtown Los Angeles for the day. The inn is also just minutes away from Old Town Pasadena and its dining and shopping district.

Each morning guests are treated to a hearty breakfast of fresh fruit, yogurt, homemade granola and a hot entrée. In the afternoon, the inn features a selection of assorted teas and sweets. After dinner at one of the neighborhood restaurants, guests can wind down with chocolates and port.

INNKEEPER: Janet Marangi
ADDRESS: 1038 Magnolia Street, South Pasadena, California 91030
TELEPHONE: (626) 799-5668; (888) 799-5668
E-MAIL: innkeeper@artsistsinns.com
WEBSITE: www.artistsinns.com
ROOMS: 7 Rooms; 3 Suites; Private baths
CHILDREN: Welcome
PETS: Not allowed; Resident pet

CHICKEN QUICHE

Makes 5 Servings

"This is a hearty quiche using egg substitute. Even the men love it!"
—INNKEEPER, *The Artists' Inn*

2 cups cooked chicken breast, chopped
1 medium onion, chopped
¼ cup celery, chopped
Dash of tarragon
¼ cup grated Cheddar or Jack cheese
¼ cup scallions
1 tablespoon all-purpose flour
¼ cup chopped, fresh vegetables (peas, broccoli, etc.)
1 unbaked pie shell
1 (4-egg) package Egg Beaters
¼ teaspoon white wine Worcestershire Sauce
1 teaspoon Dijon mustard
½ cup half & half
1 cup skim milk
½ cup chopped almonds

Preheat oven to 325°F. In a medium skillet, sauté cooked chicken, onion, celery and tarragon until vegetables are tender. Remove to a large bowl. Add cheese, scallions, flour and vegetables. Form pie shell into a quiche dish and pour in chicken mixture. In a medium mixing bowl, combine remaining ingredients and pour over chicken mixture. Bake for 1 hour.

TALLMAN HOTEL

The main building of this elegant luxury hotel was originally built in the 1890s after the first on-site hotel burned in a fire. Later, the hotel's Blue Wing Saloon fell victim to prohibition and was torn down. In 2003, owners Lynne and Bernard Butcher purchased the hotel, determined to restore its old glory. Great care was taken to re-use many of the original materials in the restoration process. Their painstaking work and dedication earned the hotel an historic preservation award from the California Heritage Council.

Guests will enjoy modern day comforts in a turn-of-the-century setting. Hand painted murals, antiques and custom furniture grace the wonderfully appointed rooms. A complimentary continental breakfast is served daily in the hotel's historic dining room and the Blue Wing Saloon and Café is open daily.

INNKEEPERS: Lynne & Bernard Butcher
ADDRESS: 9550 Main Street, Upper Lake, California 95485
TELEPHONE: (707) 275-2244; (866) 708-5253
E-MAIL: info@tallmanhotel.com
WEBSITE: www.tallmanhotel.com
ROOMS: 13 rooms; 4 Suites; Private baths
CHILDREN: Welcome
PETS: Welcome; Call ahead

Open Faced Buffalo Sliders

Makes 30 Sliders

*"We're fortunate to have J Bar S Ranch raising bison
within a few miles of the Blue Wing. It's a privilege to eat
healthy food that has been purchased locally."*
—INNKEEPER, *Tallman Hotel*

BURGERS
5 pounds ground buffalo meat
1 medium diced onion
6-10 garlic cloves, minced
1 teaspoon salt
2 teaspoons black pepper

SAUCE
1 pound white mushrooms, sliced
2 garlic cloves, minced
2 cups whipping cream
Sliced red onion, to garnish
Slivered green onions, to garnish

For burgers: Mix together all meat ingredients. Form into 1-inch thick, 2 ounce patties (makes about 30). Broil or pan-fry to rare – do not overcook.

For the sauce: Sauté mushrooms and garlic in olive oil until soft and caramelized. Slowly whisk in the cream. Reduce heat and stir until thick and creamy, about 5-7 minutes.

To serve: Place the cooked meat patty on sliced baguette. Top with sauce and garnish with onions.

FLEMING JONES
HOMESTEAD B&B

Originally the site of an 1800s cattle ranch, the Fleming Jones Homestead is now a bed & breakfast and working horse farm. World champion miniature horses are raised on-site and owners Mark and Robin Miller, both refugees of the wine industry, use their experience and expertise in the industry to make their own homemade wines from grapes grown on the premises. This elegant country setting is a great place to relax and recuperate from the daily grind. French-Swiss antiques adorn guest rooms in the main house and the bunkhouse features a western theme in honor of the old cattle ranch.

"We have traveled around the world several times and stayed in some wonderful places. But, I would have to say this is one of the most hospitable, comfortable, welcoming and fantastic places we have ever stayed in. I love the horses, dogs and especially Jasper. We will be back."

—GUEST

INNKEEPERS: Mark & Robin Miller

ADDRESS: 3170 Newton Road, Placerville, CA 95667

TELEPHONE: (530) 344-0943

E-MAIL: info@robinsnestranch.com

WEBSITE: www.robinsnestranch.com

ROOMS: 5 Rooms; 1 Suite; 1 Cottage; Private Baths

CHILDREN: Welcome

PETS: Welcome; Resident pets

Pretty Tasty Italian Sandwiches

Makes 2-3 Servings

"After spending 3 hours making breakfast every morning,
Robin no longer spends that amount of time making a gourmet
dinner very often. This fast and easy recipe came to be thanks
to a hankering for one particular Bay Area restaurant's
Italian Meatball Sandwich. Served with red wine and a salad,
it is as satisfying as the 'real thing.'"

—INNKEEPER, *Fleming Jones Homestead Bed & Breakfast*

1 red onion, chopped
1 tablespoon olive oil
5 Hot Italian sausage links, casings removed
¾ – 1 (28-ounce) can Hunt's
   Classic Italian Garlic and Herb Spaghetti Sauce
1 glass red wine
Whole wheat bread or sourdough rolls
Parmesan cheese, grated

Sauté onion in olive oil. Add sausages and break up with a spatula while cooking. Once the sausages are cooked, add the sauce and the red wine. Cover and simmer 30 minutes. Serve over toasted bread and sprinkle with Parmesan cheese.

A HAVEN OF REST B&B

Haven of Rest Bed & Breakfast is known for its warm Italian hospitality. This unique inn is dedicated to the comfort and privacy of its guests. Nestled against a fruit orchard and overlooking the sierra mountains, this wood frame home is just minutes from Yosemite National Park where guests can enjoy hiking, biking, rock climbing, white water rafting, kayaking and nature watching.

Begin your day with a sumptuous country style breakfast. In the evening, wind down with a relaxing soak in the private outdoor hot tub before you retire to the Mountain View Suite. This inn only books one party at a time and provides a great homey atmosphere for vacationing couples and families alike.

INNKEEPERS: Mike & Jody Telegan
ADDRESS: 39681 Pine Ridge Road, Oakhurst, California 93644
TELEPHONE: (559) 642-2617; (559) 779-1445
E-MAIL: jodi@sti.net
WEBSITE: www.havenofrestbnb.com
ROOMS: 2 Rooms; 1 Suite; Private baths
CHILDREN: Welcome
PETS: Welcome; Call ahead

Veal Scaloppini with Lemon

Makes 6 Servings

*"Initially, my husband's recipe called for 1 lemon.
For years I would sneak in a little extra all the while
getting rave reviews from guests. When I finally confessed,
my husband altered the recipe."*

—INNKEEPER

¼ pound butter
2 pounds veal, dredged in flour
Moderate sprinkle lemon pepper
Salt
1½ pounds mushrooms, sliced
2 whole lemons
5 packets Washington's Golden seasoning
1 cup cream sherry

Melt butter in a large sauté pan. Moderately brown the veal in the butter; season with lemon pepper and salt. Remove veal from pan and set aside. Add the sliced mushrooms to the pan and sprinkle with juice from lemons. Do not overcook. Sprinkle the Washington's Golden seasoning over the mushrooms and stir. Return veal to pan and add remaining Washington's Golden and sherry. Cover and simmer 8 minutes.

SORENSEN'S RESORT

Your all season resort in the Sierra Nevada

Sorensen's is a historic resort in the Sierra Nevada committed to providing hospitality, lodging and cuisine of the highest quality. Come hike, fish, ski, bike, raft, celebrate a wedding or anniversary or, as the resort's guests have been doing since 1926, simply refresh yourselves in the pure mountain air.

Choose from cozy cottages to fully outfitted log cabins and mountain homes. All are situated on the edge of Hope Valley, an incomparably scenic alpine setting ringed by aspens and criss-crossed by trout-filled rivers.

INNKEEPERS:	John & Patty Brissenden
ADDRESS:	14255 Highway 88, Hope Valley, California 96120
TELEPHONE:	(530) 694-2203; (800) 423-9949
E-MAIL:	info@sorensensresort.com
WEBSITE:	www.sorensensresort.com
ROOMS:	33 Cottages; Private & shared baths
CHILDREN:	Welcome
PETS:	Dogs welcome

Classic Beef Burgundy Stew

Makes 8 Servings

2 pounds beef stew meat, trimmed and cubed

1 medium white or yellow onion, diced

2 tablespoons olive oil

¼ cup butter

3 teaspoons coarse black pepper

Pinch of salt

4 tablespoons fresh, chopped garlic, divided

1½ quarts beef broth

1 quart Burgundy wine

2 bay leaves

1½ tablespoons Knoors beef base, divided

3 carrots, peeled and julienne sliced

1 small bunch celery, julienne sliced

3-4 medium white or red potatoes, quartered

2 cups mushrooms, sliced

2 tablespoons dried parsley

2 tablespoons dried basil

2 tablespoons cornstarch

½ cup water

In a medium skillet over high heat, sauté stew meat and onions in the butter and olive oil until meat is nicely browned. Add salt, pepper and 1 tablespoon of the garlic to the meat mixture. In a large stew pot, combine beef broth, wine and bay leaves and cook over medium heat until it reaches a boil. Lower heat to simmer and add meat mixture, remaining garlic and 1 tablespoon of beef base. Stir thoroughly, cover and cook for 1 hour, or until meat is tender. Add carrots, celery and potatoes and cook for another 35-40 minutes. In the last 20 minutes of cooking, add dried herbs and mushrooms. Adjust seasonings to taste and add the remaining beef base, if needed.

Dissolve the cornstarch in water and add slowly to the stew to thicken. Stir for approximately 5 minutes. Serve hot with rustic bread and salad of butter lettuce, shallots, Stilton cheese and simple vinaigrette. Leftover stew is great over wide egg noodles.

GINGERBREAD COTTAGES B&B

Gingerbread Cottages is an enchanting property on the north shore of Clear Lake featuring intimate cottages with exquisite lakefront views. Each cottage is tastefully decorated with antiques, artwork and special attention to detail. Set on a two-acre estate, this collection of themed cottages is surrounded by large oak and bay trees.

Whether you choose water sports, a swim in the pool, enjoy the large rock barbeque surrounded by flower gardens or just sit on a private deck and listen to the splash of the water, you'll find fun and relaxation.

INNKEEPERS: Yvonne & Buddy Lipscomb

ADDRESS: 4057 East Highway 20, Nice, California 95464

TELEPHONE: (707) 274-0200; (888) 880-5253

E-MAIL: mail@gingerbreadcottages.com

WEBSITE: www.gingerbreadcottages.com

ROOMS: 10 Cottages; Private baths

CHILDREN: Children age 12 and older welcome

PETS: Not allowed

Tourtière

Makes 6 Servings

"This hearty French meat pie is as much a part of the French-Canadian Christmas as "Papa Noel" (Santa Claus). This recipe was adapted from The Avon International Cookbook (1983)."

—INNKEEPER, *Gingerbread Cottages*

1 pound ground pork
½ pound ground veal
6 slices of bacon, cut up
½ cup chopped onion
½ cup chopped celery
1 clove garlic, minced
2 teaspoons dried sage, crushed
¼ teaspoon salt
¼ teaspoon pepper
1¼ cups water
2 teaspoons cornstarch
Frozen pastry dough

Preheat oven to 400°F. In a Dutch oven, brown ground pork, veal and bacon pieces. Drain off fat. Stir in chopped onions, celery, garlic, sage, salt and pepper. Stir in 1 cup of the water and bring to a boil. Reduce heat and simmer, covered, for 10-15 minutes, or until onion is tender, stirring frequently. Combine cornstarch and the remaining ¼ cup of water. Add to pot, cooking and stirring until mixture is thickened and bubbly. Cook and stir 1-2 minutes and then remove from heat.

Place one pie shell in the bottom of a 9-inch pie plate. Fill with meat/vegetable mixture and top with second shell. Cut slits in the top crust and bake 25 minutes, or until crust is golden brown. Let stand 15 minutes before serving.

DAVENPORT ROADHOUSE

B uilt on the site of the original Davenport General Store, the Davenport Roadhouse underwent massive renovations in 2006. The Davenport has since opened its doors as a restaurant, inn and store where weary travelers and locals alike stop in for great food, service and ocean-view accommodations. This eco-friendly inn and store was specially designed with both the preservation and appreciation of the environment in mind. Located just steps away from the ocean and surrounded by national park land, the Davenport Roadhouse is perfectly positioned to offer a unique lodging experience.

Guest rooms are decorated and furnished specifically to reflect the natural beauty of the area. Each room comes with an ocean-view, luxury beds and a complimentary continental breakfast that can be served in your room, at your request. Champagne, truffles and strawberries are also offered as a romantic upgrade to any room.

INNKEEPERS: Emma Rapp & Alexis Pettigrew
ADDRESS: 1 Davenport Avenue, Davenport, California 95017
TELEPHONE: (831) 426-8801 x 100
E-MAIL: info@davenportroadhouse.com
WEBSITE: www.davenportroadhouse.com
ROOMS: 8 Rooms; 1 Suite; Private baths
CHILDREN: Welcome
PETS: Not allowed

Seafood Pasta

Makes 2 Servings

"This special was so popular we had to add it to our regular menu!"

—INNKEEPER, *Davenport Roadhouse*

½ teaspoon fresh chopped garlic
½ teaspoon chopped shallots
3 scallops
3 shrimp
10 calamari
½ cup white wine
½ cup cream
3 ounce fresh mozzarella
3 roma tomatoes, diced
5 asparagus, chopped
4 ounces crab meat
1 ounce fresh herbs
    (basil, sage, thyme, oregano or parsley)
8 ounces cooked pasta
Salt and pepper to taste

In a large skillet over medium-high heat, sauté garlic and shallots in olive oil until browned. Add scallops and shrimp and cook 1 minute. Add the calamari, white wine and cream and bring to a boil. Reduce heat to medium and add mozzarella, tomatoes, asparagus, crab meat and herbs. Season with salt and pepper to taste. Allow sauce to thicken and pour over cooked pasta. Garnish with Parmesan cheese if desired.

APPLE LANE INN

Aptos, California

The Apple Lane Inn bed & breakfast is a large, warm, circa 1870 Victorian farmhouse overlooking two acres of farmland, meadows, gardens and redwood groves. Explore nearby beaches, shops, restaurants, redwood forests and wineries. Sail in beautiful Monterey Bay. Visit Santa Cruz and its famous boardwalk. Look for antiques in nearby Aptos, Soquel, and Capitola. With so much to see and do, you will not leave any time soon.

Relax in the Grand Parlor in front of a roaring fire and listen to the inn's piano player or browse the divers library of movies and books.

INNKEEPERS: Trent & Diane Wong
ADDRESS: 6265 Soquel Drive, Aptos, California 95003
TELEPHONE: (831) 475-6868; (800) 649-8988
E-MAIL: info@applelaneinn.com
WEBSITE: www.applelaneinn.com
ROOMS: 3 Rooms; 5 Suites; Private baths
CHILDREN: Welcome
PETS: Dogs & cats welcome; Resident pets

Alder-Roasted Salmon with Shrimp & Roasted Red Pepper Mousse

Makes 6 Servings

1 head roasted garlic*
10 ounces cooked shrimp meat
¼ cup heavy cream
Basil-infused olive oil
15 fresh basil leaves, chopped
    plus 30 whole fresh basil leaves, divided
Juice from ½ lemon
1 egg
¼ teaspoon sugar
2 tablespoons diced roasted red pepper
Unsalted butter
6 (6-ounce) center-cut salmon filets,
    skin removed and divided
Salt and pepper, to taste

Squeeze roasted garlic cloves into a bowl and mash into a paste. Put garlic, shrimp, cream, 1 teaspoon of basil-infused olive oil, chopped basil leaves, lemon juice, egg and sugar in a food processor. Purée for 1-2 minutes into a mousse; transfer to a chilled metal bowl. Fold in red peppers. Season with salt and pepper. (Can be prepared up to a day in advance and refrigerated.)

Spread red bell pepper mousse over 3 salmon filets. Sandwich with remaining salmon. Brush with basil-infused olive oil. Sprinkle with salt and pepper. Preheat oven to 375°F. Prepare alder plank according to package directions, brushing plank with basil-infused olive oil. Put plank on a baking sheet. Make 3 beds of 3-4 basil leaves on plank. Sprinkle with basil-infused olive oil. In a skillet over medium-high heat, sear salmon for 1 minute per side. Put salmon on basil leaf beds. Top each salmon filet with 3 basil leaves. Cover with foil and roast for 9-10 minutes. Remove salmon from oven. Let rest for 2 minutes, then remove foil. Remove salmon and basil beds to plates.

Note: To roast garlic, cut top off garlic bulb so tops of cloves are exposed. Drizzle with olive oil. Cover with foil and roast in a preheated 300°F oven for 1 hour.

OLD CROCKER INN

The Old Crocker Inn is set on the historic Crocker Ranch which was founded as a hunting retreat in the 1880s by railroad magnate Charles Crocker.

Ulysses S. Grant hunted game with the "Big Four" in these hills above the Russian River. For the last century, the Crocker Ranch has been a speakeasy, a dude ranch, a private residence and a restaurant and inn. Today the ranch is still home to an assortment of wildlife including deer, rabbits and a variety of birds.

The Old Crocker Inn offers a full breakfast, massage service and a swimming pool. Each of the eight rustic guest rooms has either a whirlpool bath or claw-foot tub, gas fireplace, an array of natural bath products and plush robes.

INNKEEPERS:	Marcia & Tony Babb
ADDRESS:	1126 Old Crocker Inn Road, Cloverdale, California 95425
TELEPHONE:	(707) 894-4000; (800) 716-2007
E-MAIL:	innkeeper@oldcrockerinn.com
WEBSITE:	www.oldcrockerinn.com
ROOMS:	8 Rooms; 2 Suites; 2 Cottages; Private baths
CHILDREN:	Welcome
PETS:	Dogs allowed; Resident pet

Smoked Salmon Crêpes

Makes 4 Servings

CRÊPES
2 eggs
½ cup sifted flour
1 cup milk
Dash Worcestershire sauce
Pinch of salt
Grated Parmesan cheese (optional)
2 tablespoons melted butter plus extra for oiling pan

FILLING
6 ounces smoked salmon, separated into small strips
1 ripe avocado, cut into thin slices
1 medium tomato, cut into ½-inch wedges

For crêpes: In a medium bowl, whisk eggs until well beaten; mix in flour, milk, Worcestershire, salt and Parmesan cheese. Add more milk if needed, add butter last. Batter should be thin. Lightly brush an 8- or 9-inch crêpe pan with butter. Heat over medium-low heat until a few drops of water skitter across the pan. Pour ⅓ cup of batter into pan and swirl to coat the bottom. Sprinkle a pinch of Parmesan cheese on the crêpe, if desired. Turn the crêpe over when lightly browned, 2-3 minutes, and cook for 1-1½ minutes to finish. Stack crêpes between layers of wax paper to prevent them from sticking together.

To assemble: Lay a layer of salmon across the middle of one crêpe (from one edge to another), follow with a layer of avocado and then tomato. Roll up and top with a dollop of crème fraîche* and a sprinkle of capers. Garnish the plate with fruit and a sprig of rosemary, or herb of choice.

*For crème fraîche: The night before preparing crêpes, whisk together ½ cup whipping cream and ½ cup sour cream until well blended. Cover loosely and place in a reasonably warm place overnight, or until thickened. The following morning, refrigerate, without stirring, for several hours. When ready to use, blend well. Mixture should be thick enough to spoon dollop onto the finished crêpe.

1859 HISTORIC NATIONAL HOTEL

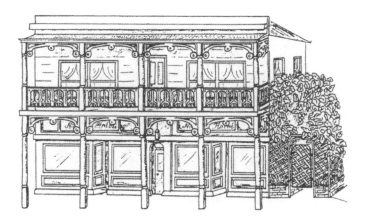

Located in Jamestown, halfway between Yosemite National Park and Lake Tahoe, this historic, California Gold Country bed & breakfast was established in 1859 and is one of the oldest continuously operating hotels in the state. Each of the award-winning, restored rooms has a wonderful brass bed, regal comforters, lace curtains and a private bath.

The highly acclaimed National Hotel Restaurant has both indoor and outdoor European style seating. The restaurant's award-winning wine list features selections from the Sierra Nevada foothill wine region.

INNKEEPER:	Stephen Willey
ADDRESS:	18183 Main Street, Jamestown, California 95327
TELEPHONE:	(209) 984-3446; (800) 894-3446
E-MAIL:	info@national-hotel.com
WEBSITE:	www.national-hotel.com
ROOMS:	9 Rooms; Private baths
CHILDREN:	Children age 10 and older welcome
PETS:	Welcome; Resident pets

Halibut with Shrimp Pâté & Apricot Glaze

Makes 8 Servings

32 ounces halibut, cut into 4 ounce pieces
½ pound (2 sticks) butter
9 ounces cold water cooked and
   peeled small bay shrimp
1 package Phyllo dough
1 tablespoon lemon juice

APRICOT GLAZE
2 cups apricot halves
3 ounce brandy
1 cup packed brown sugar

In a skillet, melt the butter and skim off excess fat; set aside. In a blender, combine shrimp and lemon juice; purée and strain off excess fluid by pressing in a towel. Unfold Phyllo dough and remove two pieces. Drizzle with melted butter and fold 2 edges toward the center; drizzle again. Place one 4-ounce piece of halibut at one end of the Phyllo dough and cover top with shrimp pâté. Roll the halibut in the dough, folding in the edges to seal. Brush entire roll with butter and place on buttered parchment paper. Refrigerate thoroughly before baking.

Preheat oven to 350°F. Bake Phyllo wrapped halibut for 15 minutes, until brown. Serve with apricot glaze.

For the glaze: In a blender or a food processor, blend all ingredients until smooth. Heat in a small skillet to serve.

Avalon,
a Luxury B&B

Imagine an enchanted forest. In a clearing, a Tudor home is nestled amidst towering redwoods. On the expansive deck, afternoon tea and cookies await. In the sunny meadow, comfortable chairs beckon. The unique décor and original hand-painted murals let you step into another world.

The exquisite suites are the ultimate place for a fantasy getaway. Amenities include king-size beds, luxury linens, down comforters and pillows, private entrances, fireplaces and large baths with steam showers and hot tubs.

INNKEEPER: Hilary McCalla

ADDRESS: 11910 Graton Road, Sebastopol, California 95476

TELEPHONE: (707) 824-0880; (877) 328-2566

E-MAIL: getinfo@avalonluxuryinn.com

WEBSITE: www.avalonluxuryinn.com

ROOMS: 3 Suites; Private baths

CHILDREN: Call ahead

PETS: Not allowed; Resident pets

Mexican Soufflé

Makes 6 Servings

"This is an Avalon favorite! Serve it with homemade pico de gallo, guacamole and chips – yum!"

—INNKEEPER, *Avalon Luxury Bed & Breakfast*

6 whole green chiles (canned)
2 cups shredded Cheddar cheese
2 cups shredded Monterey Jack cheese
12 eggs
½ cup milk
1 teaspoon ground cumin
1 teaspoon flaked dried oregano
1 teaspoon flaked dried cilantro
½ teaspoon salt
½ teaspoon pepper, to taste
1 large clove garlic, minced

Preheat oven to 350°F. Spray 3 medium scallop-edged ramekins with non-stick cooking spray. Dice the chiles and layer on the bottom of each dish. Layer ⅔ cup of each cheese in each ramekin. Combine remaining ingredients in a blender and pour ⅓ of the batter into each dish. Bake for 30-40 minutes, or until browned. Cut each soufflé into fourths and serve, two pieces per plate.

HEADLANDS INN

Indulge yourself and be pampered with warmth and hospitality at the Headlands Inn. Come and relax on a featherbed in a romantic, ocean-view room with a crackling fire and a gourmet breakfast served in your room! The Headlands Inn is a charming bed & breakfast of simple elegance, located in the heart of the historical coastal village of Mendocino. This is the perfect place for those looking for a romantic weekend getaway. If you decide to leave your rooms, the inn is just a short stroll to Mendocino's unique shops, fine galleries, superb restaurants and the mighty Pacific Ocean.

This circa 1868 New England Victorian Salt-Box once housed a barbershop, a classy 19th century restaurant and even served as extra space for the local hotel. The home was moved to its current location in the late 1800s. The six unique guest rooms each boast private baths, wood-burning fireplaces and ocean or village views. The enchanting private cottage has its own jetted tub perfect for two.

INNKEEPERS: Denise & Mitch
ADDRESS: 10453 Howard Street, Mendocino, California 95460
TELEPHONE: (707) 937-4431; (800) 354-4431
E-MAIL: innkeeper@headlandsinn.com
WEBSITE: www.headlandsinn.com
ROOMS: 6 Rooms; 1 Cottage; Private baths
CHILDREN: Children age 12 and older welcome
PETS: Not allowed

Southwestern Soufflé

Makes 1 Serving

"Taste of the Southwest made easy!
This soufflé can be made the night before, or for a last minute entrée.
It is one of our top two guest requested recipes."
—INNKEEPER, *The Headlands Inn Bed & Breakfast*

1 flour tortilla, large snack size
2 eggs
$\frac{1}{3}$ cup shredded Colby cheese,
    plus additional for serving
1 teaspoon diced green chiles
Chopped fresh cilantro
Bacon bits
Sour cream, to serve
Salsa of choice, to serve
Black olives, to serve

Preheat oven to 350°F. Spray an individual sized round soufflé dish with non-stick cooking spray. Heat tortilla in the microwave for 30-40 seconds, until soft. Press tortilla into the bottom of the dish. In a small bowl, mix together eggs, ⅓ cup of cheese and green chiles. Beat mixture well and pour over tortilla. Place a generous handful of additional cheese on top and sprinkle with bacon bits and cilantro. Bake 35 minutes, until cheese is melted and edge of tortilla is browned. Serve with sour cream, salsa and black olives.

HISTORIC REQUA INN

The Historic Requa Inn is located on the Northern California coast, in the center of Redwood National Park on the Klamath River and just a mile from the ocean. A hotel has been operating almost continuously on this site since the 1880s. Today's Requa Inn combines the friendliness and comfort of a casual bed & breakfast with the privacy and personal service of a small hotel. It is a quiet, cozy base for your redwood adventures.

Breakfast and dinner, like the inn, are substantial and without a lot of frills. The focus is on fresh ingredients – local when possible – simply prepared.

INNKEEPERS:	David & Barbara Gross
ADDRESS:	451 Requa Road, Klamath, California 95548
TELEPHONE:	(707) 482-1425; (866) 800-8777
E-MAIL:	innkeeper@requainn.com
WEBSITE:	www.requainn.com
ROOMS:	12 Rooms; Private baths
CHILDREN:	Children age 8 and older welcome; Call ahead
PETS:	Not allowed; Resident pets

Lemon Linguine

Makes 4 Servings

"With its intense lemony flavor, this pasta makes a nice side dish with fish or chicken. Or, serve it as an entrée, either as a vegetarian dish or topped with grilled prawns."

—Innkeeper, Historic Requa Inn

$^2/_3$ cup heavy cream
2 egg yolks
½ cup grated Parmesan cheese
Juice and grated zest of 2 lemons
  (a generous ¼ cup of juice)
1 pound linguine
½ stick butter
¼ cup chopped fresh parsley

Heat cream just to the boiling point in a small, heavy saucepan over medium-heat; remove from heat. In a small bowl, whisk egg yolks. Add hot cream, a dribble at a time, being careful not to curdle egg yolks. Stir in Parmesan cheese, lemon juice and lemon zest; set aside.

Cook pasta al dente. Melt butter in a large saucepan over medium heat. Add pasta and toss to coat. Add lemon mixture and toss to combine. Cook for about 1 minute, just to marry ingredients. Remove from heat. Add parsley, toss and serve.

STANFORD INN BY THE SEA

The Stanford Inn by the Sea embodies the best of the rugged Mendocino Coast. Rather than an inn with gardens, this is a small, working organic garden and farm with an inn. Yet, in the tradition of the finest inns, it offers superior guest accommodations with views of the gardens, pastures and ocean.

The Ravens, the Stanford Inn's vegetarian restaurant, features exceptional vegetarian and vegan cuisine. Selections include pizzas, salads, soups, elegant entrées and wonderful deserts that are sure to please any diner.

INNKEEPERS:	Joan & Jeff Stanford
ADDRESS:	44850 Comptche Ukiah Road, Mendocino, California 95460
TELEPHONE:	(707) 937-5615; (800) 331-8884
E-MAIL:	info@stanfordinn.com
WEBSITE:	www.stanfordinn.com
ROOMS:	32 Rooms; 9 Suites; Private baths
CHILDREN:	Welcome
PETS:	Welcome; Resident pets

Tofu Satay with Peanut Sauce

Makes 3 to 4 Servings

"This recipe is a very popular entrée or appetizer
in our restaurant, the Ravens. The tofu is skewered and grilled,
then served with a Thai-style peanut sauce."
—INNKEEPER, *Stanford Inn by the Sea*

1 (16-ounce) block firm teriyaki tofu

PEANUT SAUCE
1 tablespoon canola oil
½ cup sliced red onion
1½ teaspoons minced fresh ginger
1½ teaspoons minced fresh garlic
2 teaspoons red chile paste
¼ cup rice vinegar
1 tablespoon white sugar
3 tablespoons brown sugar
1 tablespoon tamari soy sauce
Salt, to taste
Juice of 1 lime
¼ cup cilantro leaves
½ cup coconut milk
¾ cup crunchy peanut butter

Cut tofu into 3 lengthwise slices. Grill tofu, with enough heat to
leave frill marks, until crisp. Remove from heat and cut into long,
wide strips. Skewer on skewers and serve with peanut sauce.

For the peanut sauce: Heat oil in a large skillet over medium heat.
Add onion and ginger; cook, stirring frequently, until browned.
Add garlic and chile paste; brown lightly. Add rice vinegar, white
and brown sugars, tamari, salt, lime juice and cilantro. Bring to
a boil. Add coconut milk and return to boil. Purée in a blender
or food processor. Return to heat and bring to a simmer. Slowly
whisk in peanut butter until melted and combined.

Fruit Specialties, Desserts, Cookies & Bars

Fruit Specialties, Desserts, Cookies & Bars

Life is uncertain.

Eat dessert first.

—ALICE MAY BROCK

CasaLana

CasaLana Bed & Breakfast and Gourmet Retreats is located in the charming, quaint town of Calistoga, at the top of the Napa Valley. The secluded, private setting makes it seem as if you are miles from everything when really you're just a few blocks from Calistoga's picturesque downtown, with its numerous spas, shopping and world-class restaurants.

CasaLana offers "gourmet retreats" for home cooks and food enthusiasts. Classes are taught in the inn's professionally equipped kitchen and range in length from a three-hour class to a five-day Culinary Learning Vacation.

INNKEEPER: Lana Richardson

ADDRESS: 1316 South Oak Street, Calistoga, California 94515

TELEPHONE: (707) 942-0615; (877) 968-2665

E-MAIL: lana@casalana.com

WEBSITE: www.casalana.com

ROOMS: 2 Rooms; Private baths

CHILDREN: Welcome

PETS: Not allowed

Spiced Fruit Crostata with Preserves

Makes 8 Servings

2-3 apples (can use pears, peaches, apricots, etc.), sliced
1-2 tablespoons white sugar, depending on sweetness of fruit
1-2 tablespoons brown sugar, depending on sweetness of fruit
1 teaspoon finely chopped candied ginger
½ teaspoon cinnamon
1-2 tablespoons all-purpose flour
Finely chopped lemon, orange or lime zest, to taste
½ cup preserves, such as fig, or marmalade
1-2 tablespoons Amaretto liqueur
Pie dough (homemade or store-bought) for 1 pie
Melted unsalted butter
Coarse (decorating) sugar

Preheat oven to 400°F. Put apples in a large bowl. In a small bowl, combine white and brown sugar and candied ginger. Sprinkle ⅔ of sugar mixture and cinnamon over apples; toss well to coat. Let stand for a few minutes until apples give off some of their juices. Using a sieve, sprinkle flour over apples; toss well to coat. Add lemon, orange or lime zest.

Put preserves in a small saucepan over low heat and warm slightly. Add enough Amaretto to make a spreadable, but not runny mixture. Simmer 1-2 minutes, just until well mixed. Remove from heat and cool.

Roll out dough into a ⅛-inch thick, 12-inch disk. Transfer to a parchment paper-lined rimmed baking sheet. Spread preserve mixture over dough. Sprinkle dough with ½ of remaining sugar mixture. Arrange apple slices over dough, leaving a 2-inch border around edges. Fold 2-inch border over apples to create a rim to seal in fruit and juice (make sure there are no cracks for juices to escape during baking).

Brush crust with melted butter. Sprinkle crust and exposed fruit with remaining sugar mixture. Sprinkle coarse sugar over crust. Bake for 30-40 minutes, until crust is golden brown and fruit is bubbly, rotating as needed to brown crust evenly. Remove crostata from oven and transfer to a wire rack. Serve warm.

BABBLING BROOK INN

Cascading waterfalls, a meandering brook and a romantic garden gazebo grace an acre of gardens, pines and redwoods surrounding this secluded, urban inn. Built in 1909 on the foundation of an 1870s tannery, a 1790s gristmill and a 2,000-year-old Indian fishing village, the Babbling Brook Inn is the oldest and largest bed & breakfast in the Santa Cruz area.

Rooms are decorated in styles representing the works of Old World artists and poets such as Monet, Tennyson, Degas, Cezanne and Renoir. Each has a cozy featherbed and delightful view of the gardens and brooks.

INNKEEPER: Claire Whitelaw
ADDRESS: 1025 Laurel Street, Santa Cruz, California 95060
TELEPHONE: (831) 427-2437; (800) 866-1131
E-MAIL: babblingbrook@innsbythesea.com
WEBSITE: www.innsbythesea.com
ROOMS: 13 Rooms; Private baths
CHILDREN: Welcome
PETS: Not allowed

Apple Cranberry Crisp

Makes 6 to 8 Servings

5 Granny Smith apples,
   peeled and sliced into wedges
½ cup cranberries
   (or raspberries or raisins)
¾ cup all-purpose flour
1 stick plus 2 ⅔ tablespoons butter
2 teaspoons cinnamon
¾ cup old-fashioned or
   quick-cooking oats
¼ teaspoon salt
1 cup granola
1 cup packed brown sugar
Ice cream or whipped cream,
   for serving (optional)

Preheat oven to 375°F. Fill a greased 8x8-inch baking pan with cranberries and apples. Put flour and butter in a bowl. Rub butter into flour with your hands until mixture resembles coarse crumbs. Add cinnamon, oats, salt, granola and brown sugar; combine well and sprinkle over fruit in pan.

Bake for 40 minutes, until top is browned and apples are tender (check after 30 minutes and cover with foil to prevent burning, if needed). Serve warm with ice cream or whipped cream, if desired.

Coxhead House Inn

Hidden quietly in the San Francisco peninsula's reflective past, you'll find this historic, 1891 Tudor Revival bed & breakfast that offers the rustic pleasures of days gone by. A bit of England comes alive in a leisurely atmosphere with gardens and comfortably elegant accommodations.

The home was built as a country retreat by Ernest A. Coxhead, a noted English architect. Coxhead used the English rural vernacular, with a double bowed roof and delicate, leaded glass windows to add charm to his English cottage. The home has survived, almost untouched, for over a century.

INNKEEPERS: Steve Cabrera & Pat Osborn

ADDRESS: 37 East Santa Inez Avenue, San Mateo, California 94401

TELEPHONE: (650) 685-1600

E-MAIL: innkeeper@coxhead.com

WEBSITE: www.coxhead.com

ROOMS: 5 Rooms; Private & shared baths

CHILDREN: Welcome

PETS: Not allowed

Banana Fritters

Makes 4 to 5 Servings

*"This was my grandmother's recipe. She sometimes substituted four,
thinly sliced, tart green apples for the bananas."*

—INNKEEPER, *Coxhead House Bed & Breakfast Inn*

1 egg
½ cup milk
1 cup all-purpose flour
1½ tablespoons lemon juice
1 teaspoon baking powder
3-4 tablespoons vegetable oil
4 very ripe bananas
3 tablespoons powdered sugar

In a bowl, beat egg and milk with a mixer. Gradually beat in ½ cup of flour. Beat in lemon juice. Add remaining ½ cup of flour and baking powder; beat just until blended.

Heat oil in a skillet over medium heat. Slice each banana crosswise into 3 equal pieces. Slice each piece in half lengthwise. With a fork, dip 3 banana slices at a time into egg mixture, coating thoroughly.

Gently transfer each banana piece to skillet. Cook just until golden brown on each side. Remove cooked banana slices to paper towels to drain, then quickly transfer to a warm plate. Arrange 5-6 banana slices in a flower pattern on each plate. Dust entire plate with powdered sugar and serve.

AMBER HOUSE INN

Originally built in 1905, the Amber House Bed & Breakfast Inn had been hosting discerning travelers to Sacramento since 1984. Centrally located in Sacramento's hip midtown area, the

Amber House is within walking distance of the California State Capital Building as well as a wide array of savory restaurants and chic nightlife.

As a four-diamond inn, Amber House is committed to providing guests with all the amenities of a luxury hotel and is renowned for its special pampering, warm hospitality and impeccable service.

INNKEEPERS: Judith Bommer & Kevin Cartmill

ADDRESS: 1315 22nd Street, Sacramento, California 95816

TELEPHONE: (916) 444-8085; (800) 552-6256

E-MAIL: info@amberhouse.com

WEBSITE: www.amberhouse.com

ROOMS: 10 Rooms; Private baths

CHILDREN: Welcome

PETS: Not allowed

Baked Seasoned Pear

Makes 2 Servings

"When the days get shorter and colder, we turn the fireplace on in the dining room early in the morning. This pear makes a perfect first course for breakfast during the autumn and winter months."
—INNKEEPER, *Amber House Bed & Breakfast Inn*

1 D'Anjou pear, cut in half,
    core but leave the stem on one side
2 tablespoons brown sugar
2 tablespoons unsalted butter
½ cup orange juice
Cinnamon, to taste
Nutmeg, to taste
Cloves
Dried cranberries or Craisins

Preheat oven to 335°F. Place the sugar into the bottom of a Pyrex baking dish. Lay pears flat-side-down so they are sitting on top of the sugar. Place the butter on top of the pear halves. Pour orange juice over pears and sprinkle with cinnamon, nutmeg, cloves and cranberries. Bake for 25 minutes until pear is tender and begins to brown.

Serve hot pear and juice in a soup plate and sprinkle rim with cinnamon for garnish.

GATE HOUSE INN

The Gate House Inn is a historic mansion set among landscaped lawns and gardens and surrounded by quiet and serene countryside. Go back in time as you read by imported Italian marble fireplaces or sit on expansive porches and watch for deer and wild turkeys. Sun by the large pool or simply relax and immerse yourself in the elegance of days gone by.

A full breakfast features homemade breads or muffins, chicken or turkey sausage, fresh fruit and parfaits, quiches, breakfast casseroles and, of course, the Gate House Inn specialty – baked French toast.

INNKEEPERS:	Jamie & Dave Ciardella
ADDRESS:	1330 Jackson Gate Road, Jackson, California 95642
TELEPHONE:	(209) 223-3500; (800) 841-1072
E-MAIL:	info@gatehouseinn.com
WEBSITE:	www.gatehouseinn.com
ROOMS:	2 Rooms; 2 Suites; 1 Cottage; Private baths
CHILDREN:	Children age 13 and older welcome; Call ahead
PETS:	Not allowed

Cinnamon Bakes Apples

Makes 10 to 12 Servings

"Make your guests 'apple pie' without the calories!
Guests comment that it is 'just like Grandma made."

—INNKEEPER, *Gate House Inn*

> 10-12 medium sized raw apples, cored
> Ground cinnamon
> Ground cardamom
> Miniature marshmallows (optional)
> Raisins (optional)
> 10-12 tablespoons margarine, about
> Light whipped cream (optional)
> Sugar in the raw (optional)

Preheat oven to 400°F. Place your apples in a glass baking dish with ¼-inch of water. Sprinkle apples with cinnamon and cardamom; place about 1 tablespoon of margarine in the empty core of each apple. Add mini marshmallows and raisins into the core of the apples (optional), pushing them down so that they don't protrude. Bake apples 35-40 minutes, they should be soft; cracks will form and the mixture may bubble.

Remove the apples from the oven and allow them to cool a bit. You'll want to serve them warm. Top with whipped cream and sprinkle with sugar in the raw. You could also serve these with a bit of low-fat vanilla frozen yogurt.

Dennen's Victorian Farmhouse

Originally built in 1877, Dennen's Victorian Farmhouse offers guests affordable luxury everything from the elegant linens, feather beds and fluffy towels to the incredible gourmet breakfast served in your room works to create a truly sumptuous experience you won't soon forget. Breakfasts may consist of quiches, stratas, eggs Benedict, strudels, frittatas, homemade muffins and breads and the inn's signature coffee.

Just minutes away, the historic village of Mendocino offers an eclectic mix of art galleries, shops, restaurants, museums and performing arts, set amidst the old New England charm of wooden walkways and picket fences.

INNKEEPERS: Jo Bradley & Fred Cox

ADDRESS: 7001 North Highway One, Little River, California 95460

TELEPHONE: (707) 937-0697; (800) 264-4723

E-MAIL: frednjo@victorianfarmhouse.com

WEBSITE: www.victorianfarmhouse.com

ROOMS: 9 Rooms; 2 Suites; 1 Cottage; Private baths

CHILDREN: Children age 12 and older welcome

PETS: Not allowed

Best Friends Chocolate Cake

Makes 1 Cake

*"My best friend gave me this recipe years ago.
It is something we still share often and is a family favorite.
It's a deliciously chocolaty cake that can stand on its own,
even without the coffee drizzle or, the recipe can be doubled and
made as a layer cake. The cake is vegan and is great for people with
dairy or egg allergies – though you'd never know it!"*

—INNKEEPER, *Dennen's Victorian Farmhouse*

1½ cups all-purpose flour
¼ cup unsweetened cocoa powder
1 cup sugar
Dash of salt
1 teaspoon baking soda
1 cup water
5 tablespoons vegetable oil
1 tablespoon white vinegar
1 teaspoon vanilla extract
¼ cup raisins, flaked coconut, chocolate chips
    and/or walnuts (any 1 or mixture of any or all
    totaling ¼ cup, or more to your taste)
Ice cream for serving (optional)

COFFEE DRIZZLE TOPPING
1 teaspoon instant coffee powder
Powdered sugar
2 tablespoons boiling water, about

Preheat oven to 350°F. Grease and flour a 9x9-inch baking pan.
In a large bowl, combine flour, cocoa, sugar, salt and baking soda;
mix well. Add water, oil, vinegar and vanilla; mix well. Stir in
raisins, coconut, chocolate chips and/or walnuts. Pour batter into
pan. Bake for 30 minutes, or until a toothpick inserted in center
comes out clean. Cool cake briefly, then poke holes in it with a fork
or a toothpick. Pour topping over cake. Serve warm or at room
temperature with ice cream. Great with coffee and a best friend.

For the coffee drizzle topping: Combine coffee powder, powdered
sugar and enough boiling water to form a drizzling consistency.

BLACKTHORNE INN

Blackthorne Inn Bed & Breakfast provides intimate accommodations in a rustic, beautiful setting adjacent to the magnificent Point Reyes National Seashore and an hour from San Francisco and the Wine Country. The unique structure resembles a giant, elegant tree house. Crafted from redwood, cedar and a 180-foot Douglas fur cut and milled on-site, the four-level inn rises through fragrant trees to sunny decks.

A generous buffet breakfast is served on the deck or in the glass solarium whose walls were once doors in the old San Francisco railroad depot.

INNKEEPERS:	Susan & Bill Wigert
ADDRESS:	266 Vallejo Avenue, Inverness, California 94937
TELEPHONE:	(415) 663-8621
E-MAIL:	susan@blackthorneinn.com
WEBSITE:	www.blackthorneinn.com
ROOMS:	5 Rooms; 1 Suite; Private baths
CHILDREN:	Children ages 14 and older welcome
PETS:	Not allowed

Fudge Ribbon Cake

Makes 12 to 16 Servings

2 tablespoons plus 1 stick butter, softened
¼ cup plus 2 cups sugar
1 (8-ounce) package cream cheese, softened
1 tablespoon cornstarch
3 eggs, divided
2 tablespoons plus 1⅓ cups milk, divided
1½ teaspoons vanilla extract
1½ cups all-purpose flour
1 teaspoon salt
1 teaspoon baking powder
1 teaspoon baking soda
4 ounces unsweetened baking chocolate, melted

CHOCOLATE FROSTING
¼ cup milk, plus more if needed
½ stick butter
1 cup chocolate chips
1 teaspoon vanilla extract
2½ cups powdered sugar, sifted

Preheat oven to 350°F. In a small bowl, cream 2 tablespoons of butter, ¼ cup of sugar, cream cheese and cornstarch. Add 1 egg, 2 tablespoons of milk and ½ teaspoon of vanilla; beat with a mixer at high speed until smooth and creamy. In a large bowl, combine flour, 2 cups of sugar, salt, baking powder and baking soda. Add 1 sick of butter and 1 cup of milk. Beat well at low speed. Add remaining ⅓ cup of milk, 2 eggs, chocolate and remaining 1 teaspoon of vanilla; beat at low speed for 90 seconds. Spread ½ of batter in a greased and floured 9x13-inch baking pan. Carefully spread cream cheese mixture over batter. Top with remaining batter. Bake for 50-60 minutes, or until a toothpick inserted in center comes out clean. Cook cake, then frost.

For the frosting: Combine milk and butter in a saucepan over medium heat. Bring to a boil, then remove from heat and stir in chocolate chips until melted and combined. Stir in vanilla and powdered sugar. Beat until smooth. Thin with a few more drops of milk, if needed.

ELK COVE INN

The Elk Cove Inn, originally built in 1883, opened its doors in 1963 as the first bed & breakfast on the Mendocino Coast. At its inception, the home was an executive guesthouse for the L.E. White Lumber Company, which owned much of the town at the time. Today, it is still the only inn to boast private beach access. Nestled in this tiny town of only 80 full-time residents, the Elk Cove Inn is dedicated to giving guests the most relaxing, restful and rejuvenating vacation experience possible.

'Zebo, the inn's own organic restaurant, provides a comfortable and romantic dining experience with an ocean view. Chef Jeremy Baumgartner uses fresh, organic ingredients to create exotic and delectable meals. The combination of atmosphere, quality ingredients, local wines and homemade artisan breads and pastas makes for a truly wonderful dining experience.

INNKEEPER: Dave Lieberman

ADDRESS: 3600 South Highway 1, Elk, California 95432

TELEPHONE: (707) 877-3321; (800) 275-2967

E-MAIL: innkeeper@elkcoveinn.com

WEBSITE: www.elkcoveinn.com

ROOMS: 6 Rooms; 4 Suites; 4 Cottages; Private baths

CHILDREN: Welcome

PETS: Not allowed

Moring Pie

Makes 1 Pie

"A.K.A 'Guiltless Cheesecake,'
this orange-flavored morning delight is light and airy."
—INNKEEPER, *Elk Cove Inn & Spa*

2 cups cottage cheese
4 eggs
$^2/_3$ cup sugar
2 tablespoons all-purpose flour
2 teaspoons grated orange rind
1 tablespoon orange juice
¼ teaspoon orange extract
   (or Grand Marnier)
1 teaspoon ground cinnamon
1 teaspoon nutmeg

Preheat oven to 350°F. In a large bowl, beat cottage cheese with an electric mixer on high speed for 1 minute. Add remaining ingredients and blend well. Pour into a 9-inch ceramic pie dish and bake for 50 minutes – until a knife inserted in the middle comes out dry. Refrigerate overnight. Serve chilled with a slice of fruit for garnish.

OLD MONTEREY INN

The Old Monterey Inn, a luxurious award winning bed & breakfast located in beautiful Monterey, is a great place for a romantic honeymoon getaway. Plush featherbeds, luxury linens and elegant décor have helped to earn the Old Monterey Inn a place on the Condé Nast Travel Readers Choice Gold List. The inn was also featured on the Today Show as a romantic rendezvous destination.

"Visitors are treated as houseguests, made to feel at home with such thoughtful touches as goose down comforters and pillows, breakfast in bed and sherry and crackers at 5:30 every evening."
—Bon Appetit

INNKEEPER:	Maddie, Apple, Michelle & J.J Belles
ADDRESS:	500 Martin Street, Monterey, California 93940
TELEPHONE:	(831) 375-8284; (800) 350-2344
E-MAIL:	omi@oldmontereyinn.com
WEBSITE:	www.oldmontereyinn.com
ROOMS:	6 Rooms; 3 Suites; 1 Cottage; Private baths
CHILDREN:	Children age 16 and older welcome
PETS:	Not allowed

Cream Cheese Orange Chocolate Chip Cookies

Makes 36 Cookies

3 ounces cream cheese,
  at room temperature
½ cup butter
1 cup white sugar
2 teaspoons vanilla extract
2 eggs
1 cup grated orange zest
Juice from one orange
3 tablespoons orange liqueur
2 cups all-purpose flour
1 teaspoon salt
3 teaspoons baking soda
2 cups chocolate chips
1 tablespoon dried orange peel, chopped

In a large bowl, cream together cream cheese, butter and sugar. Beat in vanilla and eggs; mix thoroughly. Add orange zest, orange juice and orange liqueur and mix until fully incorporated. In a small bowl, combine flour, salt and baking soda. Add flour mixture to cream mixture 2 cups at a time and mix well. Stir in chocolate chips and orange peel. Cover and refrigerate dough until it hardens a bit, about 30 minutes.

Preheat oven to 350°F. Drop dough by heaping tablespoons 2-inches apart onto greased cookie sheet. Bake 10-12 minutes, or until cookies are golden brown around the edges. Cool on cookie sheet 3-4 minutes then transfer to a wire rack until cool. Store in zip-lock bags or cookie jar, if they last that long!

Note: Dough freezes well and recipe can be easily doubled for larger batch.

FOOTHILL HOUSE B&B

This AAA Four Diamond inn is located in beautiful Napa Wine Country, nestled among old-growth trees; Foothill House offers comfort and luxury with a splendid view. This warm and inviting inn pampers guests with sumptuous accommodations and the individual attention of their personal concierge service. Each of the inn's four charming guest rooms has been individually decorated with country antiques, handmade quilts and color schemes to match. Guests at Foothill House are treated to indulgent amenities that include comfy robes and slippers, homemade cookies and nighttime sherry.

Foothill house serves up a mouthwatering, hearty breakfast each morning that can be enjoyed in the inn's Sunroom, outside on the terrace, or in the privacy of your own room. The late afternoon "Wine Appreciation Hour" is a favorite amongst guests.

INNKEEPER: Darla Anderson
ADDRESS: 3037 Foothill Boulevard, Calistoga, CA 94515
TELEPHONE: (707) 942-6933; (800) 942-6933
E-MAIL: info@foothillhouse.com
WEBSITE: www.foothillhouse.com
ROOMS: 2 Rooms; 2 Suites; Private baths
CHILDREN: Welcome
PETS: Not allowed

Sweet Dream Cookies

Makes 6 Dozen

"Foothill House's signature cookies were featured in Bon Appétit *magazine in 1986."*
—INNKEEPER, *Foothill House Bed & Breakfast*

1 cup (2 sticks) unsalted butter
1½ cups firmly packed brown sugar
1 egg, room temperature
1 teaspoon vanilla extract
2½ cups unbleached all-purpose flour
1 teaspoon baking soda
1 teaspoon cinnamon
1 teaspoon ground ginger
1/2 teaspoon salt
1 (12-ounce) package semi-sweet chocolate chips
1 cup chopped walnuts
1 cup powdered sugar

In a large bowl, cream butter using an electric mixer. Beat in brown sugar, egg and vanilla. In a medium bowl, combine flour, baking soda, cinnamon, ginger and salt. Blend into butter mixture. Fold in chocolate chips and walnuts. Refrigerate until dough is firm (can be prepared 1 day ahead).

Preheat oven to 375°F. Break off small pieces of dough and roll into 1-inch rounds. Dredge rounds in powdered sugar. Arrange on lightly greased baking sheets, spacing at least 2 inches apart. Bake 10 minutes. Allow to cool on baking sheet 5 minutes before transferring to wire racks. Store in an airtight container.

Captain's Inn
at Moss Landing

Enjoy wonderful waterfront views form the Captain's Inn at Moss Landing. View all sorts of wildlife including birds and harbor seals. Sit next to the river as it heads out to the sea or gaze at distant Fremont's Peak. The inn is located in the middle of the beautiful Monterey Bay, near Monterey and Santa Cruz. It is just a short walk to sandy beaches, the ocean, harbor, dining, art galleries and antique shopping.

Rooms include soaking tubs, fireplaces and fresh flowers. Breakfasts feature traditional recipes from German grandmothers.

INNKEEPERS:	Captain Yohn & Melanie Gideon
ADDRESS:	8122 Moss Landing Road, Moss Landing, California 95039
TELEPHONE:	(831) 633-5550
E-MAIL:	res@captainsinn.com
WEBSITE:	www.captainsinn.com
ROOMS:	10 Rooms; Private baths
CHILDREN:	Children age 12 and older welcome
PETS:	Not allowed; Resident pet

Double Chocolate Oatmeal Cookies

Makes 24 Cookies

"Be sure to have plenty of cold milk on hand when serving. Oatmeal and chocolate are both good for you!"

—INNKEEPER, *Captain's Inn at Moss Landing*

1½ cups sugar
2 sticks butter, softened
1 egg
½ cup water
1 teaspoon vanilla extract
1½ cups all-purpose flour
⅓ cup unsweetened cocoa powder
½ teaspoon baking soda
½ teaspoon salt
3 cups old-fashioned rolled oats
6 ounces semi-sweet chocolate chips
¼ cup chopped pecans

In a large bowl, cream together sugar and butter. Beat in egg, water and vanilla. In a medium bowl, combine flour, cocoa, baking soda and salt; add to butter mixture and mix until well blended. Stir in oats, chocolate chips and pecans. Cover and chill dough for 1 hour.

Preheat oven to 350°F. Roll dough into balls, using about 2 tablespoons of dough per ball. Bake on a non-stick cookie sheet for 10-12 minutes.

Victorian Garden Inn

The Victorian Garden Inn is an historic, circa 1870 farmhouse named for the lush English gardens surrounding it. Just a short walk from Sonoma's historic downtown plaza in Northern California's

famed Wine Country, the inn offers guests an exceptional lodging experience.

A gourmet breakfast features healthful Sonoma county products. Enjoy a tantalizing assortment of fresh fruits, scrumptious pastries and muffins, granola and local cheeses served in the dining room, the gardens or on a wicker tray delivered to your room.

INNKEEPER:	Donna Lewis
ADDRESS:	316 East Napa Street, Sonoma, California 95476
TELEPHONE:	(707) 996-5339; (800) 543-5339
E-MAIL:	info@victoriangardeninn.com
WEBSITE:	www.victoriangardeninn.com
ROOMS:	2 Rooms; 1 Suite; 1 Cottage; Private & shared baths
CHILDREN:	Call ahead
PETS:	Not allowed

Aunt Alice's Persimmon Cookies

Makes 24 Cookies

"I make these moist, chewy cookies with organic persimmons."

—INNKEEPER, *Victorian Garden Inn*

2 cups all-purpose flour
1 teaspoon baking soda
1 teaspoon cinnamon
½ teaspoon nutmeg
½ teaspoon ground cloves
1 cup white sugar
1 cup packed brown sugar
1 cup shortening
1 egg
1 cup persimmon pulp*
1 cup chopped walnuts
1 cup raisins

Preheat oven to 350°F. In a large bowl, mix flour, baking soda, cinnamon, nutmeg and cloves. In a medium bowl, mix white and brown sugar and shortening until smooth. Mix in egg. Stir in persimmon. Add persimmon mixture to flour mixture; stir to combine well. Stir in walnuts and raisins. Drop dough by teaspoonful onto a greased cookie sheet. Bake for about 12-15 minutes, until golden brown.

*Note: Persimmons are available from October to February.

PRUFROCK'S GARDEN INN

Experience the magic of Prufrock's Garden Inn, a special place tucked between the ocean and magnificent mountain wilderness in a community known for its orchards and flower fields. The surrounding beachfront town is friendly and unpretentious. For those who want a big-city feel, Santa Barbara is only ten minutes away.

The Afternoon Delight is a garden-side, two-room suite with Jacuzzi tub, two patios and Dutch doors. It is the ultimate luxury experience and is perfect for those seeking romance.

INNKEEPERS:	Jim & Judy Halvorsen
ADDRESS:	600 Linden Avenue, Carpinteria, California 93013
TELEPHONE:	(805) 566-9696; (877) 837-6257
E-MAIL:	reservations@prufrocks.com
WEBSITE:	www.prufrocks.com
ROOMS:	7 Rooms; 2 Suites; 2 Cottages; Private baths
CHILDREN:	Welcome
PETS:	Not allowed; Resident pet

Crunchy-Chewy Ginger Snaps

Makes 48 Cookies

"Guests can't leave these ginger snaps alone.
The combination of a crunchy crust and chewy center
make them an inn favorite.
The recipe came from Grandma Halvorsen."

—INNKEEPER, *Prufrock's Garden Inn*

¾ cup shortening
1 cup packaged brown sugar
¼ cup molasses
1 large egg
2¼ cups all-purpose flour, sifted
2 teaspoons baking soda
½ teaspoon salt
1 teaspoon ground ginger
1 teaspoon cinnamon
½ teaspoon ground cloves
White sugar

Preheat oven to 375°F. In a large bowl, cream together shortening, brown sugar, molasses and egg until fluffy. In a medium bowl, combine flour, baking soda, salt, ginger, cinnamon and cloves. Slowly add flour mixture to molasses mixture, stirring to combine.

Form dough into balls slightly smaller than golf balls. Roll balls in white sugar. Place balls 2-inches apart on a greased cookie sheet. Bake for about 10 minutes or until cracks show in cookies. Cool briefly, then remove from cookie sheet.

LAKEPORT ENGLISH INN

The Lakeport English Inn is comprised of a pair of historic Victorian homes wrapped around a stunning English garden. Lively rooms burst with elegance and tradition. This "glimpse of England" boasts a billiard room, whirlpool tubs and a pub. Indulge in high tea on weekend afternoons, complete with scones, Devonshire cream and strawberry jam.

You will be greeted with a tray of goodies, just as if you were arriving at your own English country house. In the evening, you will receive turndown service that includes a very British bedtime treat.

INNKEEPERS:	Karan & Hugh Mackay
ADDRESS:	675 North Main Street, Lakeport, California 95453
TELEPHONE:	(707) 263-4317
E-MAIL:	lakeportenglishinn@mchsi.com
WEBSITE:	www.lakeportenglishinn.com
ROOMS:	9 Rooms; 1 Cottage
CHILDREN:	Welcome
PETS:	Not allowed

Dingle Dangle Gingerbread Squares

Makes About 30

"These cookies are so addicting that it is essential to make only one batch."

—INNKEEPER, *Lakeport English Inn*

½ stick butter, melted
1 cup packed brown sugar
1 large egg
1 teaspoon vanilla extract
½ cup all-purpose flour
2 tablespoons old-fashioned rolled oats
½ teaspoon salt
1 teaspoon baking powder
1 cup coarsely chopped walnuts
½ cup chopped candied ginger

Preheat oven to 350°F. In a large bowl, combine butter and brown sugar. Mix in egg and vanilla. In a medium bowl, combine flour, oats, salt and baking powder; stir into butter mixture. Stir in walnuts and candied ginger.

Pour batter into a non-stick or greased 8x8-inch baking pan. Bake for 25-30 minutes (do not over bake – gingerbread should be dry on the outside and firm in the center). Cool gingerbread in pan, then cut into squares.

Deer Creek Inn

This romantic Queen Anne Victorian home will transport guests to a more simpler and peaceful time. Visitors are treated like family and made to feel at home at the Deer Creek Inn. Each afternoon, guests are welcomed to an evening social hour featuring local Nevada City wines. You can tour the inn's lovely gardens and then make your way into the city for an evening of food and entertainment. Upon returning to the inn, Ken and Eileen will treat you to a special sweet treat on the sun porch or a nightcap in the parlor to help you wind down for the night.

In the morning, a scrumptious three-course breakfast awaits you. Nevada City offers travelers a wealth of leisure activities including antique shopping, horse-drawn carriage rides, art museums, wine tastings and many different walking tours. If you are looking for something a little more demanding you can enjoy bicycling, snowshoeing, tennis, golf, hiking and swimming nearby.

INNKEEPERS: Ken & Eileen Strangfeld
ADDRESS: 116 Nevada Street, Nevada City, CA 95959
TELEPHONE: (530) 265-0363; (800) 655-0363
E-MAIL: stay@deercreekinn.com
WEBSITE: www.deercreekinn.com
ROOMS: 6 Rooms; 1 Suite; Private Baths
CHILDREN: Welcome
PETS: Not allowed; Resident pet

Deer Creek Inn Brownies

Makes 2 Dozen Brownies

"When Eileen and Ken purchased the inn,
the retiring innkeepers left this recipe behind.
Eileen tweaked a few ingredients and made it her own."

—INNKEEPER, *Deer Creek Inn*

2 cups flour
2 cups sugar
1 teaspoon baking soda
½ teaspoon salt
1 cup butter, melted
1 cup water
4 tablespoons baking cocoa
½ cup buttermilk
2 eggs
1 teaspoon vanilla extract

FROSTING
½ cup butter
3 tablespoons baking cocoa
6 tablespoons buttermilk
3¾ cups powdered sugar
1 teaspoon vanilla
1 cup chopped nuts

Preheat oven to 350°F. In a medium bowl, sift together flour, sugar, baking soda and salt. Set aside. In a saucepan over medium heat, mix together butter, water and cocoa and bring to a boil. Stir in dry ingredients; add buttermilk, eggs and vanilla. Bake in a greased and floured 9x13-inch baking sheet for 20-25 minutes. Allow brownies to cool completely before topping with frosting. Cut into squares and serve.

For the frosting: In a saucepan over medium heat, mix together butter, cocoa and buttermilk; bring to a boil. Stir in powdered sugar, vanilla and chopped nuts.

SAN LUIS CREEK LODGE

The San Luis Creek Lodge is a charming bed & breakfast that offers guests all the amenities of a luxury hotel. Each of the 25 guest rooms, spread over 3 lodges, is specially decorated to create a relaxing and welcoming atmosphere. All of the rooms feature high ceilings, private baths with dual sinks, fluffy robes, Aveda bath products, in-room coffee selections as well as microwaves and refrigerators. Complimentary breakfast is included with your stay.

Located in San Luis Obispo County, the San Luis Creek Lodge is just minutes away from the downtown district and the public trolley stops right at the inn. The central location finds the inn just a short drive from many of the county's attractions including three different beaches, Hearst Castle, local wineries, gourmet restaurants and championship golf courses.

INNKEEPER:	Patty Oxford
ADDRESS:	1941 Monterey Street, San Luis Obispo, California 93401
TELEPHONE:	(800) 593-0333 x 210
E-MAIL:	info@sanluiscreeklodge.com
WEBSITE:	www.sanluiscreeklodge.com
ROOMS:	25 Rooms; Private baths
CHILDREN:	Welcome
PETS:	Not allowed

Lodge Brownies

Makes 12 Brownies

"We serve these each afternoon for arriving guests.
Many sneak back to the lobby and take the whole plate!"
—INNKEEPER, *San Luis Creek Lodge*

3-4 packs graham crackers, crushed
1 (14-ounce) sweetened condensed milk
¾ cup walnuts, halves or pieces
¾ cup chocolate chips
½ teaspoon salt

Preheat oven 325°F. In a medium bowl, combine all ingredients until moist. Spoon mixture into an 8x8-inch baking pan and bake 20-30 minutes, or until golden brown.

" *What you eat standing up*

doesn't count. "

—BETH BARNES

NAPA INN

The Napa Inn is comprised of two, adjacent, Victorian houses. The main house is a beautiful Queen Anne Victorian that was built as a wedding gift in 1899. Next door sits the Buford House, a Victorian built in 1877, which is on the National Register of Historic Places. Today, the inn retains the charm and romantic aura of its origins, with fireplaces and spa tubs in many of its rooms. A large, gourmet breakfast, served by candlelight, awaits guests in the morning.

Located on a quiet street in historic downtown Napa, the inn is within an easy stroll of shops and fine restaurants. Local attractions include: golf, wine tours, hot air ballooning, COPIA, the Napa Valley Opera House and the Napa Valley Wine Train. Relax in the quiet gardens with an afternoon refreshment, or sip a glass of port next to the cozy fire in the parlor.

INNKEEPER: Brooke & Jim Boyer
ADDRESS: 1137 Warren Street, Napa, California 94559
TELEPHONE: (707) 257-1444; (800) 435-1144
E-MAIL: info@napainn.com
WEBSITE: www.napainn.com
ROOMS: 9 Rooms; 4 Suites; 1 Cottage; Private baths
CHILDREN: Call ahead
PETS: Dogs welcome; Call ahead

Apricot Shortbread

Makes 8 Servings

1½ cups coarsely chopped dried apricots

1 stick butter, softened

1⅓ cups all-purpose flour, divided

⅓ cup plus ⅔-¾ cup sugar

¼ cup water

1 large egg, beaten

¼ teaspoon salt

½ teaspoon baking powder

Powdered sugar, for garnish

Soak apricots overnight in hot water to cover. The next day, preheat oven to 375°F. Combine butter, 1 cup of flour and ⅓ cup of sugar; mix with a spoon or your hands until smooth. Pat dough over bottom of 9-inch pie pan. Bake for about 25 minutes, or until golden brown.

Drain apricots. Combine apricots and water in a skillet over high heat. When mixture begins to bubble, lower heat to medium. Cook, stirring often (so fruit doesn't scorch), until mixture thickens. Remove from heat and cool. When cool, add egg to apricot mixture and mix well.

In a bowl, combine ⅔-¾ cup of sugar (depending on sweetness of apricots) with remaining ⅓ cup of flour, salt and baking powder; beat until smooth. Spread apricot mixture over crust and bake for 25 minutes, or until puffy. Remove from oven and cool slightly. Dust with powdered sugar. Cut into wedges and serve.

FLORA VISTA INN

 Located between Santa Cruz and Monterey, nestled among lush flower and strawberry fields and a short walk from spectacular beaches, lies a restored 1867 farmhouse offering romantic rooms, sweeping vistas and tournament quality clay tennis courts. Whether you take advantage of the world-class amenities and events the Monterey Bay has to offer, or simply wish to curl up with a good book in front of the fire, Flora Vista Inn awaits you.

The inn offers hearty breakfasts and afternoon refreshments daily and box lunches are available to guests with 24 hours' notice.

INNKEEPERS: Ed & Deanna Boos

ADDRESS: 1258 San Andreas Road, La Selva Beach, California 95076

TELEPHONE: (831) 724-8663; (877) 753-5672

E-MAIL: info@floravistainn.com

WEBSITE: www.floravistainn.com

ROOMS: 5 Rooms; Private baths

CHILDREN: Children age 12 and older welcome

PETS: Not allowed

Flora Vista Inn Granola Bars

Makes 9 Servings

*"Our guests often take strolls on the beach or
even get in a few sets of tennis before breakfast.
We developed theses granola bars to be a tasty
and nutritious snack and they are gluten-free
for out wheat sensitive guests. Many guests ask
for more at check-out and even mention them
when booking return visits."*

—INNKEEPER, *Flora Vista Inn*

½ cup butter, melted
1 cup dark brown sugar
1 egg
Dash of salt
½ teaspoon cinnamon
1½ cups quick-cook oats
½ cup old-fashioned oats
1 teaspoon baking powder
3 tablespoons dry roasted,
   slivered almonds
⅓ cup raisins

Preheat oven to 350°F. In a large bowl, combine melted butter,
brown sugar, eggs, salt and cinnamon; mix well. Add oats, baking
powder, almonds and raisins, mixture will be dry. Press mixture
into a well-greased 8x8-inch baking pan. Bake 25-30 minutes.
Remove from oven and allow to cool completely. Cut into 9 bars
and wrap well.

OLALLIEBERRY INN

The Olallieberry Inn is a historic bed & breakfast located in the seaside village of Cambria on California's central coast. The home, built in 1863, sits on Santa Rosa Creek. A 120-year-old redwood tree greets guests, and lush, colorful gardens can be enjoyed from the back deck.

In the afternoon, enjoy complimentary local wine and sumptuous hors d'oeuvres, such as baked Brie in puff pastry with toasted almonds, goat cheese and roasted garlic with freshly baked focaccia or crab paté. And, of course, there is an endless supply of home-baked cookies.

INNKEEPERS:	Marjorie Ott & Marily & Larry Draper
ADDRESS:	2476 Main Street, Cambria, California 93428
TELEPHONE:	(805) 927-3222; (888) 927-3222
E-MAIL:	info@olallieberry.com
WEBSITE:	www.olallieberry.com
ROOMS:	8 Rooms; 1 Suite; Private baths
CHILDREN:	Children ages 5 and older welcome
PETS:	Not allowed

Olallieberry Bars

Makes 12 Bars

*"We sometimes serve these bars as an afternoon treat or
when we have groups staying at the inn.
They are a favorite of our guests."*
—INNKEEPER, *Olallieberry Inn*

1 cup butter
1 cup packed brown sugar
1½ cups flour
1½ cups rolled oats
1 teaspoon baking soda
½ teaspoon salt
1 cup chopped nuts
1 (10-ounce) jar Olallieberry preserves
  (or any berry preserves)

Preheat oven to 250°F. Melt the butter in a saucepan and remove
from heat. Stir in brown sugar until it is dissolved. Cool to room
temperature. In a large bowl, combine flour, oats, baking soda
and salt; remove 1 cup of mixture and set aside for topping. Add
the butter mixture to the flour mixture and mix well. Mix in nuts
and press mixture into a greased 9x13-inch baking pan. Spread
preserves over the top and sprinkle the reserved 1 cup of flour/oat
mixture over the top. Bake 30 minutes. Cool on a wire rack and
cut into bars.

California Originals

COBB SALAD

This salad was said to have been invented at the Brown Derby restaurant in 1937. Story has it that owner, Robert H. Cobb, prepared the salad as a late night snack for the owner of Grauman's Chinese Theater. The salad has been a signature menu item ever since.

SOURDOUGH BREAD

Although sourdough bread did not originate in California, it was the main bread being baked in Northern California during the days of the Gold Rush. San Francisco sourdough bread is the most famous sourdough variety in the United States. Many bakeries still use the traditional recipe from over a century ago.

GREEN GODDESS SALAD DRESSING

Popular stories claim that this signature green dressing was invented in 1923 by the executive chef at the Palace Hotel in San Francisco. The dressing was first bottled and mass-produced in the 1970s and can still be purchased in regional stores.

FRENCH DIP SANDWICH

It is not clear exactly which L.A. restaurant invented this yummy concoction, but the sandwich definitely originated in California in 1908. Both Philippe's and Cole's Pacific Electric Buffet claim to be responsible for the creation. Although the sandwich is traditionally served with au jus on the side, for dipping, the original was prepared "wet" or already soaked, with extra on the side. Baguette bread and thinly sliced beef are the two main components of the French Dip, cheese is optional.

CALIFORNIA ROLL

This inside-out sushi roll, made with cucumber, imitation crab meat and avocado, is said to have been created by Ichiro Mashita, sushi chef at L.A.'s Tokyo Kaikan in the 1970s. The avocado was meant to be a substitute for toro, a variety of tuna. Kaikan also wrapped the roll with the rice on the outside, rather than the traditional way with nori, or seaweed, on the outside. The roll eventually made its way throughout the states in the 1980s and is partially responsible for sushi's popularity in the United States today.

Cuisine of California

California is a mecca for food lovers. The temperate climate and location make it the perfect place for a variety of fresh and organic ingredients including avocados, artichokes, dates, salmon and Dungeness crabs. Thanks to its diverse population, California has been one of the nation's forerunners in what is known as fusion cuisine, or the combination of elements from a variety of culinary traditions

Sourdough Bread

Makes 1 loaf

PLAN AHEAD.
Sourdough starter needs between 2 and 5 days for preparation.
Starter must then be allowed to proof for no less than 8 hours.

STARTER
2 cups warm water
1 tablespoon active dry yeast
2 cups all-purpose flour

BREAD
1 tablespoon butter
½ cup milk
1 teaspoon salt
1 tablespoon sugar
2 cups proofed starter
3 cups all-purpose flour

For starter: In a 2-quart bowl or jar, dissolve yeast in warm water; gradually stir in flour. Cover container with a clean washcloth and allow to sit in a warm place. Stir mixture once a day, leaving covered the remainder of the time. Your starter is ready when bubbling has subsided and the mixture has a sour/yeasty smell and mixture is slightly thickened. Starter can be refrigerated until use. To proof your starter, 8 hours prior to baking bread, mix 1 cup starter with equal parts warm water and flour (about 1 cup each) and allow to sit 8-12 hours – intensity of sour flavor will depend on how long you allow it to sit.

For bread: Preheat oven to 85oF. In a small bowl, melt butter and mix with milk; add salt and sugar and allow to dissolve. In a large bowl, combine proofed starter and milk mixture; mix well. Add flour, one cup at a time, and mix until fully incorporated. Turn dough out onto a floured surface and knead until dough is smooth. Shape dough and place in a greased baking pan. Cover with a damp cloth and allow to rise in oven until dough has roughly doubled in size (between 1½ and 3 hours).

Preheat oven to 375°F. Bake bread 10 minutes then decrease oven temperature to 350°F. Bake 30-40 minutes until crust is desired color – darker color will be a crustier bread.

Cobb Salad with Mustard Vinaigrette

Makes 2 Servings

2 cups iceberg lettuce, chopped

2 cups romaine lettuce, chopped

½ cup watercress, minced

2 tomatoes, chopped

½ pound cooked bacon, crumbled

2 boneless skinless chicken breasts,
   broiled and chopped into 1-inch pieces

2 hard boiled eggs, chopped

2 Haas avocados, chopped

½ cup Roquefort cheese

2 tablespoons chives, minced

MUSTARD VINAIGRETTE

$^2/_3$ cup good olive oil

$^1/_3$ cup red wine vinegar

1 tablespoon quality Dijon-style mustard

For salad: In a medium bowl, mix together iceberg and romaine lettuces and minced watercress; divide evenly between two large plates. Divide tomatoes, bacon, chicken breasts, eggs, avocados and Roquefort evenly among the two plates, being careful not to mix together – note that in a traditional cobb salad, the toppings are not mixed; you should divide your plate into $^1/_6$ths and making a section for each individual topping over the lettuce. Sprinkle with chives and top with basic mustard vinaigrette.

For dressing: With a hand mixer, mix together olive oil, red wine vinegar and mustard until you get an emulsified dressing. You can jazz up the dressing with any or all of the following, to taste: chopped garlic, lemon juice, Worcestershire sauce, salt, pepper and sugar - lemon juice coupled with red wine vinegar will add acidity to the dressing and the sugar would balance this out a bit.

Geographical List of B&Bs

Gold Country & High Sierra (continued)

Sanger	Sequoia View Winery Bed & Breakfast	116
Sonora	Sterling Gardens Bed & Breakfast	150
South Lake Tahoe	Black Bear Inn	148
Springville	Springville Inn	214
Sutter Creek	Hanford House Bed & Breakfast Inn	160
Twain Harte	McCaffrey House	100
Visalia	The Ben Maddox House Bed & Breakfast	138
Yuba City	Harkey House	184

Northern California

Boonville	Anderson Creek Inn	62
Calistoga	Brannan Cottage Inn	146
Calistoga	CasaLana	256
Calistoga	Chelsea Garden Inn	172
Calistoga	Foothill House	274
Calistoga	Mount View Hotel & Spa	206
Chico	Goodman House Bed & Breakfast	84
Chico	The Grateful Bed	136
Cloverdale	Old Crocker Inn	242
Elk	Elk Cove Inn & Spa	270
Eureka	Carter House Inns	114
Eureka	Cornelius Daly Inn	158
Ferndale	Shaw House Inn Bed & Breakfast	22
Forestville	Case Ranch Inn Bed & Breakfast	92
Forestville	Farmhouse Inn & Restaurant	182
Guerneville	Applewood Inn	48
Healdsburg	Camellia Inn	174
Inverness	Blackthorne Inn	268
Inverness	Ten Inverness Way	94
Kenwood	Birmingham Bed & Breakfast	144
Klamath	Historic Requa Inn	250
Lakeport	Lakeport English Inn	282
Little River	Auberge Mendocino	50
Little River	Dennen's Victorian Farmhouse	266
Little River	Glendeven Inn	26
Little River	Inn at Schoolhouse Creek	32
Mendocino	Alegria Oceanfront Inn & Cottages	60
Mendocino	Brewery Gulch Inn	218
Mendocino	Headlands Inn Bed & Breakfast	248
Mendocino	Joshua Grindle Inn	72
Mendocino	MacCallum House Inn & Restaurant	108
Mendocino	Stanford Inn by the Sea	252
Napa	1801 First	200
Napa	Arbor Guest House	86
Napa	Beazley House Bed & Breakfast Inn	82
Napa	Candlelight Inn Bed & Breakfast	74
Napa	Churchill Manor	122
Napa	Hennessey House	36

Alphabetical List of Inns

Recipe Index

Also Available from 3D Press

High Altitude Baking
$14.95 / 192 pages / ISBN 978-1-889593-15-9

The Bed & Breakfast Cookbook Series

New England Bed & Breakfast Cookbook
(CT, MA, ME, NH, RI, & VT)
$19.95 / 320 pages / ISBN 978-1-889593-12-8

North Carolina Bed & Breakfast Cookbook
$19.95 / 320 pages / ISBN 978-1-889593-08-1

Pennsylvania Bed & Breakfast Cookbook
$19.95 / 304 pages / ISBN 978-1-889593-18-0

Virginia Bed & Breakfast Cookbook
$19.95 / 320 pages / ISBN 978-1-889593-14-2

Washington State Bed & Breakfast Cookbook
$19.95 / 320 pages / ISBN 978-1-889593-05-0

New Titles in Summer 2008

Georgia Bed & Breakfast Cookbook
$19.95 / 296 pages / ISBN 978-1-889593-19-7

Florida Bed and Breakfast Cookbook
$19.95 / 296 pages / ISBN 978-1-889593-00-0

Also Available from Big Earth Publishing

High Altitude Baking

Patricia Kendall, editor

Put an end to your high altitude baking frustrations today. With over 200 recipes and proven tips developed by high altitude baking experts, this book will ensure your high altitude baking success. A cake recipe adjustment guide for bakers living at an elevation of 3,500 and 10,000 feet is included in this essential cookbook. *High Altitude Baking* includes recipes for cookies, cakes, muffins, coffee cakes, scones, biscuits, pancakes, yeast breads, sourdough breads, and more.

Paper I 6 x 9 I 192 pages I $14.95
ISBN: 978-1-889593-15-9

Recipe Please

Favorite Recipes from Colorado Restaurants

Edited by Marty Meitus

Mart Meitus, food editor of the *Rocky Mountain News*, has compiled 365 scrumptious recipes from her "Recipe, Please" column—which appears every Saturday in the Homefront section—bringing 90 Colorado restaurants into the home kitchen.

Paper I 8 x 8 I 256 pages I $16.00
ISBN: 978-1-55566-332-2

The Best of Simply Colorado Cookbook

The Colorado Dietetic Association

Emphasizing flavor, convenience, and lower-fat alternatives— the best recipes from the first two volumes.

Hardcover – wire binding I 6 x 9   304 pages I $19.95
ISBN: 978-1-56579-575-4

Palm Springs Flavors

Henry Fenwick and Eric Wadlund, Photography by Tony Tornay

The best of desert eating with recipes from the area's chefs.

Hardcover I 9.5 x 9 I 176 pages
Full-color throughout I $27.95
ISBN: 978-1-56579-582-2

3D Press Order Form

3005 Center Green Drive, Suite 220 • Boulder CO 80301
800-258-5830 • www.bigearthpublishing.com

Please Send Me	Price	Quantity
Southern Church Suppers	$19.95	_____
High Altitude Baking	$14.95	_____
California Bed & Breakfast Cookbook *(available Summer 2008)*	$19.95	_____
Georgia Bed & Breakfast Cookbook *(available Summer 2008)*	$19.95	_____
New England Bed & Breakfast Cookbook	$19.95	_____
North Carolina Bed & Breakfast Cookbook	$19.95	_____
Pennsylvania Bed & Breakfast Cookbook	$19.95	_____
Texas Bed & Breakfast Cookbook	$19.95	_____
Virginia Bed & Breakfast Cookbook	$19.95	_____
Washington State Bed & Breakfast Cookbook	$19.95	_____

Subtotal $ _____

Add $5.00 shipping for 1st book add $1 for each additional book $ _____

Total Enclosed $ _____

Send To

Name _____

Address _____

City /State/Zip _____

Phone _____ Gift from _____

We accept checks and money orders. Please make checks payable to Big Earth Publishing.

Please charge my **VISA**   **MASTERCARD**   **AMEX**   **DISCOVER**
(circle one)

Card Number _____

Expiration Date_____